# The Republic of China and U.S. Policy

# The Republic of China and U.S. Policy

*A Study in Human Rights*

A. James Gregor
Maria Hsia Chang

Ethics and Public Policy Center
Washington, D.C.

**THE ETHICS AND PUBLIC POLICY CENTER**, established in 1976, conducts a program of research, writing, publications, and conferences to encourage debate on domestic and foreign policy issues among religious, educational, academic, business, political, and other leaders. A nonpartisan effort, the Center is supported by contributions (which are tax deductible) from foundations, corporations, and individuals. The authors alone are responsible for the views expressed in Center publications. The founding president of the Center is **Ernest W. Lefever.**

**Library of Congress Cataloging in Publication Data**
Gregor, A. James.
  The Republic of China and U.S. policy.
  Includes bibliographical references and index.
    1. United States — Foreign relations — Taiwan.
2. Taiwan — Foreign relations — United States. 3. Civil rights (International law) 4. Civil rights—Taiwan.
I. Chang, Maria Hsia. II. Title.
E183.8.T3G73   1983    327.73051249    83-14130
ISBN 0-89633-073-7

**$7.00**

# Contents

# Foreword

THE DECLARATION OF INDEPENDENCE asserts the self-evident truth "that all men are created equal; that they are endowed by their creator with certain unalienable rights; that among these are life, liberty, and the pursuit of happiness; that to secure these rights, governments are instituted among men." The Founding Fathers also said that "whenever any form of government becomes destructive to these ends, it is the right of the people to alter or to abolish it" in favor of one that restores basic rights. They warned, however, that prudence dictates "that governments long established should not be changed for light and transient causes."

Recent debate over the place of human rights in domestic and foreign policy has often neglected the Founding Fathers' wisdom, born of experience and prudence. These men were not utopians; their civic virtue combined dedication to ideals with a healthy respect for circumstances and a recognition of the human condition (read "original sin"). Today's human rights crusaders are prone to two errors: they expect too much too soon, and they fail to take fully into account extenuating circumstances.

The American experiment drew upon a rich tradition of respect for human dignity and the rule of law, including the Judeo-Christian heritage, Greek philosophy, Roman law, and the Magna Charta. Even with this legacy, and without an entrenched system of feudalism or despotic rule, we were painfully slow in achieving full equality before the law. After the stirring assertion of "certain unalienable rights" in the Declaration, many decades passed and much anguish was suffered, including a civil war, before the American republic extended fundamental rights to all its citizens.

Throughout our history, our leaders have recognized that under emergency conditions, when the security or the very survival of the state is in jeopardy, certain rights may be temporarily suspended. A classic example is Abraham Lincoln's suspension of *habeas corpus* during the war to save the Union. Thousands of persons were arrested on suspicion and were imprisoned for a while, usually without a trial. In defending his action Lincoln said: "Are all the laws, *but one,* to go unexecuted, and the government itself go to pieces, lest that one be violated? Even in such a case, would not the official oath be broken, if the government should be overthrown . . .?" (quoted in Carl Sandburg, *Abraham Lincoln: The Prairie Years and the War Years* [Harcourt, Brace, 1954], p. 248).

If our robust democracy with its auspicious beginning has been long in codifying basic rights and under national emergencies has suspended some of these rights, surely we should be tolerant of the imperfect records of other states whose circumstances have been far more difficult. Most societies have no democratic tradition and are governed by authoritarian regimes. Many are under assault by domestic or foreign enemies. And some are under siege by totalitarian regimes that do not shrink from using terror, subversion, disinformation, blackmail, guerrilla war, or outright aggression to overthrow established governments.

There is a profound moral and political difference between an authoritarian regime and a totalitarian one. The former permits a significantly greater degree of freedom and diversity than the latter, and guarantees a limited range of rights. Under a totalitarian regime, no countervailing forces are permitted to challenge the status quo. There is no freedom of speech, and even the freedom to remain silent is severely restricted. The self-anointed and self-perpetuating elite are the arbiters of orthodoxy in every sphere— political, economic, academic, artistic, familial, and religious. In dealing with the ultimate questions of the nature and destiny of man, the ruling party of a totalitarian regime usurps the place of God.

Some of the zealous human rights crusaders of recent years overlook the all-important distinction between authoritarian and totalitarian regimes. The policies derived from their shortsighted insistence on an absolute standard and their selective application of these policies have done little to further the cause of freedom and justice in the world and may even have had the opposite effect in some cases. Most observers agree that American human rights activists were partly responsible for the overthrow of the Shah in Iran and Somoza in Nicaragua; in both states the new order is more corrupt and a greater violator of human dignity than the one it replaced.

The vast difference between the quality of life possible under a totalitarian government and that possible under a less than fully democratic government is strikingly evident when one compares the People's Republic of China with the Republic of China on Taiwan. In this thoughtful and richly documented analysis, Professors A. James Gregor and Maria Hsia Chang address U.S. human rights policy by focusing on the Republic of China. They understand the distinction between totalitarian and authoritarian regimes, and they recognize that Communist China poses a massive threat to the impressive measure of freedom, justice, and prosperity achieved by Republic of China though its people do not enjoy the full range of human rights guaranteed in a mature democracy. The authors affirm realistic principles of international politics and give practical policy guidelines for dealing with authoritarian regimes under siege not only in Asia but throughout the world.

A. James Gregor is the principal researcher for the Pacific Basin Project of the Institute of International Studies at the University of California (Berkeley), and a professor of political science at the university. His most recent book is the forthcoming *The Iron Triangle: An American Security Policy for Northeast Asia.* Maria Hsia Chang is an associate specialist at the Institute of International Studies and an assistant professor of political science at the University of Puget Sound. Professors Gregor and Chang are co-authors of other works, including *The Taiwan Relations Act and the Defense of the Republic of China* (with Edwin K. Snyder, 1980) and *Ideology and Development: Sun Yat-sen and the Economic History of Taiwan* (with Andrew Zimmerman, 1981).

The current study is enriched by a selective China chronology emphasizing post-1949 developments and by an appendix consisting of the sections on the People's Republic of China and the Republic of China from the 1982 State Department *Country Reports on Human Rights Practices.*

We have retained the traditional English spelling for most Chinese names. The new spelling is used for a few current names, such as Deng Xiaoping, however, and is used throughout the Appendix.

We wish to express our appreciation to several scholars who served as critical reviewers of this book in the manuscript stage: Ralph Clough, Ray S. Cline, and Richard C. Thornton, all of Washington, D.C., and Jeanne Tchong Koei Li, president of the Pacific Cultural Foundation in Taipei. As in all publications of the Ethics and Public Policy Center, the facts selected and the conclusions reached are the responsibility of the authors alone.

This study is the second of the Center's Pacific Area Project, following *America's Stake in the Pacific* by Paul Seabury (1981). It is published with the hope that it will stimulate a greater understanding of the mutual economic and security interests of the United States and its allies in the Western Pacific.

ERNEST W. LEFEVER, *President*
Ethics and Public Policy Center

Washington, D.C.
July 4, 1983

# China Chronology From 1895

## To 1949

| | |
|---|---|
| 1895 | Island of Taiwan transferred from China to Japan at end of Sino-Japanese War. |
| 1911-12 | Revolution in China, led by Sun Yat-sen; Manchu dynasty overthrown; republic proclaimed with Sun Yat-sen as president. |
| 1912 | Kuomintang (Nationalist Party) organized. |
| 1921 | Chinese Communist Party founded. |
| 1924-27 | Nationalists and Communists collaborate in attempt to free China from warlord rule and foreign occupation and bring it into modern age. |
| 1925 | Death of Sun Yat-sen. |
| 1926 | Chiang Kai-shek emerges as successor to Sun; becomes commander-in-chief of Nationalist army. |
| 1927 | Kuomintang under Chiang Kai-shek purges Communists; protracted struggle between Nationalists and Communists begins. |
| 1935 | Mao Tse-tung takes control of Chinese Communist Party. |
| 1937 | Civil war temporarily suspended because of Japanese aggression against Manchuria. |
| 1937-45 | War with Japan; Chiang's Nationalist forces greatly weakened; Communists under Mao do not participate, but build their own strength. |
| 1943 | Chiang Kai-shek becomes president of Republic of China (ROC). |

| | |
|---|---|
| 1946 | Republican constitution adopted; civil war between Nationalists and Communists resumed. |
| 1947 | Island of Taiwan restored to China after defeat of Japan in World War II. |
| 1949 | People's Republic of China (PRC) established in Peking with Mao Tse-tung as chief of state, Chou En-lai as premier; Nationalists transfer government to Taiwan. |

## *After 1949: Republic of China (ROC)*

| | |
|---|---|
| 1950 | JANUARY: U.S. announces it will no longer help Nationalists withstand attack by PRC. JUNE: North Korea invades South Korea; U.S. asks ROC to join resistance to Communist aggression, sees Taiwan as critical to defense of Asia. |
| 1955 | U.S. ratifies mutual defense treaty with ROC; U.S. Formosa Resolution empowers President to use U.S. forces against any attack on Taiwan. |
| 1971 | U.S. announces "two-China" policy regarding U. N. membership. |
| 1972 | Chiang Ching-kuo, son of Chiang Kai-shek, becomes premier. |
| 1975 | Death of Chang Kai-shek. |
| 1978 | Chiang Ching-kuo becomes president with Sun Yun-suan as premier. |
| 1978 | U.S. recognizes PRC, ceases to recognize ROC. |
| 1979 | U.S. enacts Taiwan Relations Act: it will continue to treat Taiwan as an independent nation while acknowledging the claim made by both Peking and Taipei that Taiwan is sovereign Chinese territory; U.S. will continue to sell arms to Taiwan, conduct the equivalent of consular functions, and maintain cultural and economic ties. |

## *After 1949: People's Republic of China (PRC)*

| | |
|---|---|
| 1949-58 | PRC makes substantial economic progress with Soviet help. |
| 1958 | Mao Tse-tung abandons Soviet economic model and proclaims Great Leap Forward, with disastrous results; resigns as chief of state, gives post to Liu Shao-ch'i. |
| 1959-65 | Liu Shao-ch'i dismantles Great Leap Forward program and reestablishes more conventional economic measures. |
| 1965-66 | Mao accuses Liu of betraying socialism and taking capitalist road; mobilizes youth as Red Guards. |
| 1966-69 | Cultural Revolution; activities of Mao's Red Guards plunge China into chaos, cut it off from outside world, and nearly destroy its economy. |
| 1972 | President Nixon visits PRC; U.S. and PRC issue Shanghai Communiqué in which U.S. acknowledges there is only one China. |
| 1976 | Death of Premier Chou En-lai and of Chairman Mao; Hua Guofeng becomes premier and party chairman. |
| 1977 | Deng Xiaoping becomes vice premier and assumes powerful political role. |
| 1978 | U.S. recognizes PRC, ceases to recognize ROC. |
| 1979 | Vice Premier Deng visits U.S. |
| 1980 | Zhao Ziyang replaces Hua Guofeng as premier. |
| 1981 | Hu Yaobang replaces Hua Guofeng as party chairman. |

CHAPTER ONE

# Human Rights in Totalitarian and Authoritarian Systems

*The struggle between liberty and totalitarianism is indeed an asymmetrical one and always has been; and so far as I can see, our human rights policy has only trivially added to the sum of justice in the world while at the same time adding incalculably to the already burdensome handicaps of the liberty party. . . . In this context, the argument about whether we can distinguish between authoritarianism and totalitarianism is little more than a moral smoke screen. Making such a distinction is not only necessary to, it is the moral enterprise itself. Anyone who is not a moral cretin can and does make these distinctions whether he admits it or not.*

MIDGE DECTER, 1981[1]

IT IS NOW GENERALLY CONCEDED that the Carter administration's embrace of human rights as the "central focus" of American foreign policy produced very little of substance. There is scant evidence that it did much to relieve the suffering of individuals, groups of individuals, or entire nations that found themselves deprived of fundamental rights.

Not least of the many reasons for this failure was the fact that the United States had precious little influence over those international political actors who were the prime violators of human rights. Washington did, however, penalize some lesser offenders who happened to be real or potential allies. In 1977, military assistance

1

to Argentina, Ethiopia, and Uruguay was terminated or reduced. Subsequently, Brazil, El Salvador, Guatemala, (pre-Sandinista) Nicaragua, and (post-Allende) Chile were reported to have similarly suffered. The Congress of the United States cut $5 million from the aid package to the Republic of the Philippines at a time when Manila was struggling with a rural insurrection led by the Maoist New People's Army.

In effect, Jimmy Carter's human rights policies were often selectively applied, simply because the United States could exercise little influence where influence was most needed. And the countries that did suffer this influence were almost always allies of the West. The consequence was that those Western allies, organized to contain the spread of revolutionary Communism with all its egregious violations of human rights, endured serious impairments, while Communism, about which Jimmy Carter said he no longer entertained "inordinate fears," enjoyed a cost-free advantage.

Any effort to make "internationally recognized human rights" the central concern of foreign policy is intrinsically flawed. In the first place, those rights that are now "internationally recognized" include so wide a range of social and economic *demands*—such as the "right" to clean air, adequate nutrition, and environmental protection—that any government seeking to satisfy all of them would find itself hopelessly bogged down. The effort to determine which "rights" should take precedence in any given circumstances would produce impossibly complex deliberations.

The traditional Western concept of human rights embraces *political and civil rights*—the rights of free speech, free association, and protection against arbitrary governmental interference in one's activities. Having secured those rights, free men can negotiate *social and economic demands*.

Recently, some governments have insisted that the pursuit of man's most "fundamental" social and economic "rights"—the "rights" to food, shelter, and employment—entails the circumscription of political and civil rights. The argument is that in order to satisfy the basic needs of "all," the rights of "some" must be sacrificed. Many of the new nations that have become members of the United Nations are prepared to acknowledge the cogency of such an argument.

However persuasive that argument may appear, it seems most unlikely that governments will rush to satisfy needs unless citizens are free to express their demands. The history of the twentieth century shows that the governments that claim to provide the most "fundamental human rights" are governments that not only deny their citizens political and civil liberties but also are among the least competent in providing social and economic benefits. East Germany provides both fewer civil and political rights and fewer social and economic benefits than West Germany. North Korea provides fewer political and civil rights than does South Korea, and also less economic well-being. Communist China gives its people far less in civil and political rights than the Republic of China on Taiwan—and dramatically less in economic and social welfare.

A fundamental problem afflicting the human rights policy of the Carter administration was that for any such policy to work, some order of priority among "internationally recognized human rights" would have to be established. Once established, each right would have to be defined with enough precision that violations could be clearly identified. Furthermore, there should be some assurance that when such violations occurred, the cases would be adjudicated by an arbiter who was understood to be competent, independent, and objective. In the international arena, none of these requirements has ever been met.

Whatever the legal status of internationally recognized human rights, the discussions of them in the United Nations have produced neither a relatively complete and coherent body of norms nor any body of norms that, however incomplete and incoherent, is binding on member states. Many major states have not ratified the covenants and conventions that contain the norms. And most of the states that *have* ratified them have not committed themselves to the reporting and complaint procedures recommended, nor agreed to abide by the deliberations of any adjudicative body. This suggests that there is no generally held view of what the ratification of a human rights covenant might mean in practice to any given signatory. Furthermore, the texts in which the catalog of human rights appears do not provide for their own interpretation, and consequently they defy adjudication.[2]

The United Nations has dealt with human rights violations almost exclusively by vote in the General Assembly. This explains why Western international legal theorists have often denied that U.N. decisions have a "legally binding character." The obligations imposed upon signatory states by U.N. conventions and resolutions turn on how critical terms in those documents are defined by a membership whose judgments will depend on the political interests and transitory concerns of the two-thirds majority of the General Assembly. What result are political, rather than legal, actions.[3]

## Two Conceptions of Law

Western legal tradition conceives law as universal in character and disinterested in application. Agencies that undertake actions or render judgments designed to serve the interests of one or another participant in a dispute do not make, adjudicate, or administer law. Their efforts are political activities that serve some extralegal purpose.   Contrasting with this essentially Western tradition is one that denies that *any* law is *ever* objective or disinterested. All law, domestic or international, it is argued, invariably serves the interests of one or another party in a dispute. According to this conception, law is only one of a number of devices used by some collection of self-interested agents in the systematic pursuit of their own interest. Marxist theoreticians, the major spokesmen for this view, insist that law is nothing other than the will of an economically defined class translated into authoritative jargon. Law is the official language of some special interest group, the "bourgeoisie" or the "proletariat," the "imperialists" or the "oppressed." What ultimately counts is power—either the power of the "privileged elites" or that of the "revolutionary people." Law is simply power expressed through legal terminology.[4]

Fundamental to the disputes about human rights in the United Nations is this difference in the conception of law. For the non-Marxist, on the one hand, law is a deliberative system that inspects, without bias, claims and counterclaims advanced by any and all parties to a dispute. It attempts an objective evaluation of the grounds tendered to support one claim against another—it is a procedural and rational process by which conflicting claims can be argued and settled.[5] For Marxists, on the other hand, law is little more than a means by which those armed with power and advantage can mystify and confuse the weak and disadvantaged—or an instrument to be used in the class struggle, a weapon to be employed to defeat a class enemy.

In one of his earliest works, *The German Ideology*, Karl Marx insisted that law was merely the official expression of the collective will of a dominant class. When productive processes generate a dominant class of persons, "the individuals who rule in these conditions . . . have to give their will, which is determined by these definite conditions, a universal expression as the will of the state, as law—an expression whose content is always determined by the relations of this class, as the civil and criminal law demonstrates in the clearest possible way."[6] Law is the "juridical expression of class relations"—it is the impersonal and idealized defense of exploitative relations.[7] The common interests of the dominant class, rendered impersonal and idealized, thus find expression in law.[8] The body of law governing *capitalist* society, in this view, reflects the fact that "the bourgeoisie, in general all the members of bourgeois society, are forced to constitute themselves . . . as a moral person, as the state, in order to safeguard their common interests."[9]

Law, domestic or international, must necessarily serve as an instrument of class struggle.[10] Consequently, when the Marxists came to power in Russia, they were disposed to treat all law as "class law," a body of sanctioned conventions designed to insure the dominance of one class over another.[11] The suggestion that the law could function as an objective arbiter in disputes between individuals or groups was dismissed as a "bourgeois fiction." For the Marxists, the state is an "organization for the maintenance of class domination."[12] The rules governing social behaviors, as well as the sanctions that sustain them, are designed to serve the collective interests of the dominant social class.[13] If the bourgeoisie is dominant, law serves the interests of the bourgeoisie. Under "the dictatorship of the proletariat, law becomes a determinate means of control exercised by society, that is to say, by the socially dominant class in society,"[14] the proletariat.

But in a Marxist society, it is not the proletariat as a whole but the "core" of the proletariat that exercises control. According to article 126 of the Soviet constitution of 1936, the "Marxist-Leninist party" must provide the "guidance of the working masses," and this has become the fundamental principle of Marxist political systems.[15] Marxist parties, invoking this principle, have maintained control over the states they have conquered, using law as one of their principal instruments.

Whatever rights are accorded individuals in a Marxist state must necessarily reflect the will of the dominant class *as that will finds expression in the decisions of the "core" elements,* the "vanguard party" of the proletariat. In the language of Soviet theoreticians, the state, which is "the representation of the will of society as a whole," discovers "the political trend of this will . . . embodied [in] the leading role of the working class, and the guiding functions of the . . . Party."[16]

If a revolutionary leadership, having wrested control of the state, accepts the notion that law is simply the "manifestation of class will" as expressed exclusively through the deliberations of a self-selected "core" or "vanguard party," it creates the preconditions for *ideocracy* and the legal foundations for *totalitarianism.* An *ideocracy* is a political system that bases its legitimacy on the purported truth of its ideology, such as "Marxist-Leninist thought," or the "thought of Mao Tse-tung." All political systems are to some extent ideological; i.e., they are based on ideas. Democratic systems, for instance, are rooted in such ideas as the rule of law, respect for human dignity, and limited government. But *ideocratic* systems are built on a narrow and rigid set of ideas or propositions, and their legitimacy rests on the absolute acceptance of these ideas, at least by the ruling elite. In democratic systems, by contrast, legitimacy rests on the free suffrage of the citizens.

A *totalitarian* system is based on the conviction that the interests of the individual are (or should be) identical with those of the state; this eliminates, in principle, all distinctions between individual privacy, the special concerns of society, and the purposes of the state. In such an environment there are no rights other than those that the state grants. The state, in effect, "may define with its own laws, from a sovereign will, the rights and duties of its nationals. . . . The problem of 'human rights' . . . remains . . . within the scope of the domestic jurisdiction of the state."[17]

Individual and collective human rights are therefore defined in terms of the interests of the socially dominant class—or, more precisely, its interests as interpreted by that class "core" or "vanguard" (article 6 of the 1977 constitution of the Soviet Union; article 2 of the 1978 constitution and the preamble to the 1982 constitution of the People's Republic of China). The "democratic dictatorship" determines what human rights are to be accorded its citizens—and those rights are expressly limited by "duties" whose "essence is the duty of protecting the . . . economic, social, and political system."[18]

## TWO CONCEPTIONS OF GOVERNMENT

As a consequence, totalitarian political systems are fundamentally different from "pluralistic" ones.[19] In pluralistic systems, the members of society are said to have some inherent human rights that law is designed to protect. A conflict between the individual and the state is adjudicated in an adversary proceeding in which the individual and his rights are defended by counsel of his choice and in which the law attempts to insure impartiality, equality, and equity. In such a situation there are understood to be certain civil and political rights that cannot be diminished. The principal agency charged with the defense of those privileged rights is an independent and effective judiciary.

The difference between ideocratic and pluralistic systems is evident in their constitutions. Ideocratic constitutions, in our own time, are generally modeled on the Stalin constitution of 1936. They are not understood to be contracts between an aggregate of individuals possessed of civil and political rights and the government they create. They are rather documentary celebrations of the accession to power of a revolutionary elite. They are ideological manifestoes—informed by the "thought of Marx," or of Lenin, or Mao—designed to protect and enhance established governmental power, rather than charters of limitations on that power. The state is understood to be the originator of rights, granting such rights to the individual with the explicit proviso that they be exercised only insofar as they "strengthen, support, and defend" the prevailing system (article 50 of the 1977 constitution of the Soviet Union; article 56 of the 1978 constitution and article 51 of the 1982 constitution of the People's Republic of China).

Under constitutions common to pluralistic systems, in contrast, individuals who make up society have inherent civil and political rights, only parts of which—as little as possible—they contract away in order to serve the necessities of government.

Almost all constitutions declare themselves "democratic" in some sense, with sovereign power ultimately vested in "the people." But only a few are animated by a conviction that individuals have some inherent and inalienable rights that do not proceed from the state. These constitutions therefore provide for legal procedures that protect these basic rights—usually freedom of expression, religion, and association and the right to privacy—from governmental caprice, and that allow an opposition to operate and thus to influence the government's allocation of social and economic benefits. Such constitutions generally provide for restraint on the concentration of governmental power through a separation of powers; they also restrict the invasion of individual civil and political rights by providing for a process of judicial review by an independent magistrature.[20]

Under these provisions, individuals and groups of individuals have found a propitious environment in which they may pursue private interests and may try to increase their access to social and economic benefits, such as occupational opportunities and social services. These individual and collective efforts to acquire increased benefits are derived from, and dependent upon, protected civil and political rights. In other words, social and economic rights are fostered and negotiated in an open, competitive political marketplace insured by the prior protection of political and civil rights.

Ideocratic constitutions, by contrast, are thought to "consolidate" the "people's power," rather than to guarantee the rights of the individual citizen. Such constitutions characteristically require that citizens "not infringe upon the interests of the state" and "refrain from any activity likely to jeopardize the interests of the . . . fatherland."[21] The constitution is understood to be the concrete expression of some sort of collective will with which the individual will is supposedly identical.[22] Under such a notion, any constraint on government would constitute a constraint on the "real will" (as distinct from the "alienated will") of the individual citizen. Any effort to provide for individual rights, as distinguished from collective rights, is understood as a "counterrevolutionary" attempt to impair the march toward some officially favored political, social, or economic goal.[23]

What civil and political rights mean in such a system is made clear in the expositions of Marxist legal theorists. For instance:

It is but natural that the right of assembly and association contains the right of the working masses to form organizations of a political nature, but it is also clear that it does not belong to the content of the right of assembly and association . . . that the working masses, the citizens of the state, create organizations against the . . . state.[24]

## The People's Republic of China

All of this has been perfectly obvious to the citizens of the People's Republic of China. The more articulate among them have lamented that "for the last thirty years," the mainland of China has suffered a system that is fundamentally "undemocratic in nature." (These and the other quoted phrases in this paragraph are from a 1979 Chinese dissident publication.) The political authorities have succeeded in creating a "dictatorship" that not only has "undermined the people's economic potential" but also has "encroached upon the people's rights." For under the constraints imposed by its ideocratic and totalitarian constitution, there is "no right to express one's opinion—no freedom of speech," no "right of assembly," no assurance that citizens can enjoy even "the most fundamental guarantee for their lives." Under such circumstances "there is no law worthy of the name."[25]

In such a political system "the notion that individuals might have rights against their social group, society, or the state [is] an utterly alien concept," as a U.S. government report puts it.[26] Millions have perished in such systems, and hundreds of thousands have languished for years, without benefit of trial, in labor camps.[27] On the mainland of China an entire nation was forced to suffer, for over thirty years, a legal system that did not have a formal criminal code or a criminal procedure code.[28] Only recently has an effort been made to separate criminal investigation, prosecution, and sentencing from the regular administrative and security functions of the Chinese Communist party—and it is still not at all clear that party organizations have stopped their arbitrary intervention in all phases of the judicial process.[29] If the 1980 trial of the notorious Gang of Four in Peking was considered by some "a step toward greater individual freedom in China," it was viewed by others as compelling evidence that the new "reformist" leadership will continue the massive violation of individual rights in the pursuit of political purpose.[30]

Subsequent to the trial of the Gang of Four, authorities in Peking have continued to violate almost every article of the U.N. International Covenant on Civil and Political Rights. In the arrest of political dissidents on the notoriously vague charge of "counter-revolutionary activity," the rights embodied in articles 18 and 19 of the covenant, designed to protect the freedom of conscience, speech, and expression, were violated. The vagueness and ambiguity of the charges for which the dissidents were arrested also violated article 15 of the covenant, which affirms that "no one shall be held guilty of any criminal offense on account of any act or omission which did not constitute a criminal offense, under national or international law, at the time it was committed."[31] Articles 9 and 14 of the U.N. covenant, meant to insure public trial and adequate defense for individuals, were systematically violated in the detention of the dissidents and in the proceedings through which they were sentenced and incarcerated. In fact, Amnesty International characterized this entire period, after the trial of the Gang of Four and after the introduction of a criminal code and a criminal procedure code, as one marked by "a noticeable deterioration in the human rights situation."[32]

In Communist China, the violation of political rights has been accompanied by an entire constellation of equally serious violations of the rights of individual privacy, religious freedom, mobility, and integrity (i.e., freedom from physical and mental abuse).[33] It is against this background that the 1982 constitution as a reaffirmation of the "Four Basic Principles" announced in 1981 for the political governance of Communist China must be understood. On February 23, 1981, Chang Yu-yu, deputy secretary general of the Constitutional Revision Committee of the People's Republic of China, insisted that under any constitutional revision, the Communist party of China must insure the security of the "people's democratic dictatorship," the primacy of the Party, the prevalence of "Marxism–Leninism–Mao-Tse-tung Thought," and the pursuit of the "socialist road." Any revision of the constitution must reaffirm the "leadership of the Party"; the constitution must be framed in such a way as to implement "the line and the specific and general policies of the Party."[34]

In an ideocratic system, an ideologically inspired governing elite arrogates to itself the right to determine the freedoms to be accorded the vast majority of citizens. Charged with the obligation of acting out the injunctions buried in the crabbed prose of the "universal geniuses" of Marxism, the ruling minority grants its subject constituency only those civil and political rights that "support and strengthen the system." What follow, predictably, are impairments of human rights ranging from systematic invasions of privacy to mass murder.

Thus the impressive catalog of human rights dutifully recorded in ideocratic constitutions is invariably qualified by the priority given to party rights and interests, which are understood to represent the "real and ultimate will" of the collective people. The constitution of the Soviet Union, like that of the People's Republic of China and that of socialist Cuba, does not set forth legal prohibitions ordained by the sovereign people against the power of government; rather, it contains descriptive affirmations of the conditions of human rights permitted by the sovereign state. Other than the proclamation of rights, always qualified by a defense of the prevailing system, there is no provision that the laws themselves or the applications of the laws can ever be judicially reviewed by a body with any independence from the "leading and guiding force" behind the state, i.e., the Party. There is no recourse for individual citizens against abuse by officialdom, since there is no authority other than the government itself to which they can appeal.

Ideocratic systems in our time are wedded to the conviction that international law, no less than domestic law, is "the aggregate of various norms . . . expressing the will of the ruling classes."[35] International law "reflects only the will and need of the ruling class of big capitalist powers."[36] Thus the "class struggle" is transposed to the international arena, and "bourgeois" international law is pitted against "proletarian" international law. The two types are "opposite in character, and they serve the policy of different classes."[37]

## Two Conceptions of Human Rights

In such circumstances, any notion of internationally recognized human rights must necessarily come to grief in the attempt to accommodate the presumed differences in "class" perspectives and "class" interests between international parties. The entire history of human rights, as those rights have been respected and abused, testifies to the fundamental differences between pluralistic and ideocratic systems. In sum, the human rights arena has become the battleground for two fundamentally different conceptions of government, with the Soviet Union and the People's Republic of China the principal spokesmen for one and the United States and its close allies the principal spokesmen for the other. The difference turns on a basic disagreement about the nature of human rights. For ideocratic systems, the entire notion of "privileged" and "inherent" human rights is an elaborate "bourgeois fiction." For the democratic powers, the concept of "inherent human rights" represents an argued judgment that to treat some civil and political rights as inherent accords critical protection for the individual against the superior strength of the state and permits a system to be responsive and flexible in meeting its people's needs.

When President Carter announced his proposed human rights policy, he said this policy would have the advantage of not being burdened by an "inordinate fear of Communism." This suggests that Carter had fundamentally misunderstood what was at stake. Clearly, U.S. policies should not be freighted with any "inordinate" fears; but any serious human rights policy would have to recognize that Communist systems intrinsically violate human rights as the West understands those rights.

Whatever the abuses in the non-Communist authoritarian systems of Argentina, (pre-revolutionary) Nicaragua, El Salvador, the Republic of South Africa, and the Republic of Korea in recent years, they pale into relative insignificance in the face of the enormities that have tortured the populations of the Communist states of Laos, Kampuchea (Cambodia), Vietnam, the People's Republic of China, and Cuba. In these latter countries, millions have been forced to flee their homes and millions remain in labor camps. More than a million—perhaps more than two million—were murdered under Pol Pot's revolutionary ministrations.

More than that, the infractions of authoritarian regimes have almost always been violations *in practice,* while those in Communist totalitarian regimes have been violations *in principle.* Many persons have refused to acknowledge this significant distinction. When authoritarians in Chile, Turkey, Greece, or South Korea violate civil or political rights, their actions are almost always characterized as "temporary" derogations. Such authoritarians themselves acknowledge that their behavior is exceptional; there is a clear recognition that such infringements can be warranted only by extraordinary circumstances. There is a "postponement" of democracy, a "suspension" of civil and political rights. However much their behaviors are to be deplored, such regimes at least pretend to share common ground with the West. Therefore the United States has often been in a position to negotiate the restoration of "suspended" rights and an increase of freedoms once the emergency conditions are mitigated.

In closed ideocratic systems, however, human rights cannot be restored, because the very notion of inherent human rights is treated as a perverse fiction. The exercise of free speech and political opposition in such systems, for example, is itself understood to violate the human rights of a "whole people," whose rights are defined in terms of the ideology of the elite party.

The Carter administration, which either did not recognize or did not acknowledge these differences, exercised "selective outrage." The sanctions at its disposal were directed mainly against authoritarian regimes, often allies of the West. Against the Communist regimes, which were the most fundamental violators of civil and political rights, the Carter policy had no effective sanctions. Toward the end of his tenure in office, for lack of any alternatives, Jimmy Carter was employing "quiet diplomacy" to attempt to influence Communist regimes. The massacres in Pol Pot's Kampuchea were scarcely acknowledged—until those horrors had become the object of universal concern.

But more than that, the Carter administration's treatment of authoritarian, non-Communist regimes was never guided by any clear operational criteria. In its response to human rights violations, no distinction was made between violations that derived from fundamental government policy, as might be the case in traditional absolute monarchies, and those that were the consequence of special emergency conditions, as when a constitutional democracy had to contend with grave internal and external threats to its security. A human rights policy is gravely flawed if it fails to distinguish between violations undertaken simply to insure the security of office for self-serving felons, and violations undertaken in the cause of defense against systemic threats to the well-being of the entire population.

## THREE TYPES OF REGIMES

Any American human rights initiative must recognize three major types of regimes: (1) open, competitive, and pluralistic systems, which require little attention; (2) non-competitive, mostly revolutionary Marxist, elitist, ideocratic systems, upon which American policy has little direct impact; and (3) "authoritarian" regimes that range from simple political obscenities like that of Idi Amin, through military juntas and traditional monarchies, to regimes that appear to be attempting to move from semi-competitive to mature competitive systems. It is this last class, semi-competitive systems, that is most susceptible to international influence. For the revolutionaries in Moscow and Peking, these systems are almost all "bourgeois" and "reactionary," and Marxist strategies anticipate their transformation into analogues of Communist Cuba or socialist Vietnam. Communist revolutionaries will make every effort, through diplomatic pressure or covert operations, to undermine their viability. The treatment by the United States of these semi-competitive systems may very well determine whether they collapse under revolutionary pressures into non-competitive, ideocratic "people's democracies" or are able to progress to more responsible forms of government.

The Carter administration gave little evidence that it recognized this distinction, though it is of substantial importance in the matter of human rights. It seems perfectly obvious that a unified Vietnam under Communist rule offers far less freedom than did the authoritarianism of Diem or Thieu so much deplored by many human rights activists—and Communist rule also offers far less of a prospect for ameliorative change. That a unified Korea under the Communist rule of Kim Il Sung would enjoy more human rights than a South Korea under Chun Doo Hwan is most unlikely. And any suggestion that the Kampuchea of Pol Pot provided more human rights than the Cambodia of the authoritarian Lon Nol would be an outrage.

It is neither in the best interests of the United States nor consonant with our concern for human rights to drive members of the semi-competitive class into the formally closed and non-competitive class. It would therefore be derelict for the United States to insist upon immediate conformity to some ideal standard of human rights in semi-competitive systems whose survival is threatened. Even the most severe of authoritarian regimes, in principle, remains open to American and other foreign influence, while ideocratic systems do not.

One consequence of the relative openness and vulnerability of semi-competitive systems is that more will be heard about their human rights abuses than is ever heard about those of closed systems. While there was immediate international outrage over human rights violations in post-Allende Chile and in Argentina, almost nothing was heard about the massacre of between one-seventh and one-third of the entire population of Kampuchea, or about the three million who were killed and the 100 million who suffered massive violations of their rights in the People's Republic of China during the tragic years of the "Great Proletarian Cultural Revolution," until long after the events.[38]

Those who shape U.S. foreign policy must therefore make it clear that their initiatives cannot be solely the consequence of public outcry. The relative abundance of information about human rights restrictions in South Africa will arouse the wrath of the public while the dearth of information about violations in mainland China will insure that these pass virtually unnoticed. Almost everyone laments the wretchedness of the displaced Arabs of Palestine, but almost no one anguishes for the quarter of a million Laotians forced to flee their homes by their "revolutionary" Marxist government.

Public pressure must influence the deliberations of America's foreign policy establishment, but that establishment must have independent criteria that allow it both to make a convincing public response to such concerns and to develop policies that display coherence and fidelity to the defense of human rights.

## The Republic of China on Taiwan

To find out what is involved in developing such criteria, we will look closely at one member of the class of semi-competitive, authoritarian regimes—the Republic of China on Taiwan (ROC).

There is a great deal of confusion about the nature of the ROC. Many Americans identify it as "free China," to distinguish it from the Communist People's Republic of China (PRC). Some American intellectuals classify the ROC as "reactionary" and the mainland regime as "progressive."[39] The U.S. government officially recognizes that the ROC is one of those authoritarian systems that Henry Kissinger identified as "morally distinct" from those that are intrinsically non-competitive.[40] The U.S. government lauds the achievements of the ROC; it also regularly enumerates the violations of human rights that occur there.[41] The ROC is now a diplomatically "derecognized" but "friendly" power with whom we share a "special relationship." It is one of the regimes over which the United States has exercised, and continues to exercise, considerable influence.

Like many other nations, the Republic of China has undertaken a program of intensive economic development and has suffered all the attendant tensions. Unlike many developing nations, however, the ROC has not lapsed into totalitarianism or simple bestialities. The political leadership in Taipei has led the Republic of China from the privations of 1945 to the relatively open and manifestly wealthier and more egalitarian society of today. It affords an instructive instance of the evolution of an authoritarian political system into a more democratic one.

Any sensible policy calculated to further human rights will have to reckon with the world's imperfections—and with the threats and tensions with which the world abounds. Otherwise it will take on an abstract and unreal quality, as though the sole consideration should be the satisfaction of some ideal standard of performance. It can be said that even in the most advanced democratic systems the full flowering of human rights has not yet been achieved. The best we can expect from any community is progress in the direction of the ideal. This is the kind of realistic expectation that has motivated the best of our human rights activists.

CHAPTER TWO

# Emergency Regimes in Democratic States

*It would be a miscarriage of justice for a norm with its derivative to be interpreted and applied mechanically or in disregard of common sense and the facts of the case. . . . A less than absolute commitment to political freedom is implied by Article 4 of the [International] Covenant on Civil and Political Rights. Its language authorizes the signatories during emergencies threatening the life of the nation to derogate "from their obligations under the present Covenant to the extent strictly required by the exigencies of the situation."*

KURT GLASER and STEFAN T. POSSONY, 1979[1]

ALMOST ALL DEMOCRATIC CONSTITUTIONS contain emergency clauses—that is, provisions for the government to suspend, for a specified period, some essential civil and political rights of its citizens. Such rights can be restored by emergency regimes because, though suspended or restricted during the period of emergency, these rights are still held to exist; they are not abolished. In Marxist-Leninist and Maoist systems (and their analogues), by contrast, rights are *not* understood to have an inherent existence; they exist only to the extent that they support the state and its institutions. For an emergency regime of a constitutionally established democratic system, the abridgment of individual human rights is viewed as an abnormality; in noncompetitive regimes, it is a permanent feature of the system.

For twenty-one months between 1975 and 1977, India imposed emergency measures that suspended almost the entire range of civil and political rights. At the close of the period, however, those rights were restored. Greece, similarly, has suffered intervals of emergency rule but has ultimately returned civil and political rights to its citizens. The Philippines operated under emergency regulations from 1972 until 1980. South Korea periodically lapses into emergency rule but later restores civil and political rights.

Governments impose emergency rule because they believe that the survival of the state or the safety and well-being of its citizens is in jeopardy. The state of martial law imposed upon the Philippines in 1972 was explained in this way:

> It . . . [has been] established that lawless elements moved by common or similar ideological conviction . . . and employing the active, moral, and material support of a foreign power, and being guided and directed by intensely devoted, well-trained, determined, and ruthless groups of men, and seeking refuge under the protection of our constitution and liberties to promote and attain their aims, have entered into a conspiracy and have in fact joined and banded their resources and forces together for the prime purpose of, and in fact they have been and are actually staging, undertaking, and waging, an armed insurrection and rebellion against the Government of the Republic of the Philippines in order to forcibly seize political and state power in this country, overthrow the duly constituted government, and supplant our existing political, social, economic, and legal order with an entirely new one whose form of government, whose conception of God and religion, whose notion of individual rights and common relations, and its political, social, economic, legal, and moral precepts, are based on Marxist-Leninist-Maoist teachings and beliefs . . . [Proclamation 1081, September 26, 1972].[2]

In the face of this emergency, the president of the Philippines, by virtue of the powers vested in him by the constitution (art. 7, sec. 10, par. 2), declared the republic to be under martial law. Suspects were administratively detained for a period whose length was determined by the military authorities. A nationwide curfew was imposed between midnight and 4 A.M. Public assemblies were banned, and the movements of individuals were restricted. To bear arms without explicit military approval was considered a capital offense (subsequently reduced to a serious felony). The public information media were placed under government control.

The necessity of emergency regimes, which tend to have the same general features, is now well established in domestic and international law. The European Convention for the Protection of Human Rights and Fundamental Freedoms, perhaps the best formulated code protecting human rights in international law, allows restrictions on civil and political rights "in time of war or other public emergency threatening the life of the nation . . . to the extent strictly required by the exigencies of the situation . . ." (art. 15[1]). This coincides with article 4 of the European Convention on Civil and Political Rights, and corresponds in substance to article 4 of the U.N.'s International Covenant on Civil and Political Rights, which affirms:

> In time of public emergency which threatens the life of the nation and the existence of which is officially proclaimed, the States Parties to the present Covenant may take measures derogating from their obligations under the present Covenant to the extent strictly required by the exigencies of the situation. . . .

The right of collective self-preservation has been traditionally acknowledged as the most fundamental right in the law of nations. Both international law and customary practice provide for the exercise of emergency powers that limit political and civil rights in circumstances understood to threaten the survival of the nation.

But there has been no compelling definition of an emergency grave enough to "threaten the life of the nation." In the two cases in which the European Court of Human Rights was asked to rule on the use of emergency clauses in the European Convention for the Protection of Human Rights and Fundamental Freedoms, the court supported the authorities against individual petitioners.

The European Court held that the term "public emergency threatening the life of the nation" should be broadly construed to refer to an "exceptional (and imminent) situation of crisis and emergency which affects the whole population and constitutes a threat to the organized life of the community of which a State is composed."[3] But the questions remain: Who is to judge when an emergency is great enough to warrant serious limitations on civil and political rights? And who is to decide the extent of the limitations required?

The European Court advised that in judging the decision to invoke emergency powers the observer must put himself "in the position of the person or persons whose acts are judged, and . . . investigate—setting aside any emotional or personal considerations—whether those persons had manifestly behaved unreasonably or arbitrarily."[4] In effect, this means that emergency measures are to be judged by the standards of right reason and proportionality. Right reason and proportionality are held to exclude absolutely the arbitrary taking of life, the use of torture as administrative practice, and retroactive punishment. These violations of human rights are proscribed by almost every international document devoted to the protection of individuals. But aside from these clear restrictions, emergency powers can be exercised insofar as they are "compatible with reality" and "commensurate with the magnitude of the emergency." They are to be used only to avoid some greater evil and are to be administered not only in good faith but in the spirit of the rule of law.

## Emergencies in Canada, Ireland, Northern Ireland

Most democratic regimes, even the most stable, have at one time or another made use of emergency powers. On October 16, 1970, Prime Minister Pierre Trudeau proclaimed a "state of apprehended insurrection" throughout Canada. Citing the kidnapping of a Canadian minister and a British consul by members of the Front for the Liberation of Quebec (FLQ), he invoked the War Measures Act, authorizing extraordinary powers of arrest, search, and detention. Four hundred and fifty suspects were arrested, and although most were never charged with any offense, many were held incommunicado for a considerable time. The emergency decree effectively suspended the Canadian Bill of Rights. On December 4, 1970, the prime minister of the Republic of Ireland declared that a "grave emergency" existed in his country. On the basis of information that a splinter group of the Irish Republican Army was conspiring to kidnap "prominent" state officials, he said he was prepared to empower the police to "intern any citizen without trial" for the duration of the emergency.

Usually emergency powers are limited to a specific period of crisis. At times, however, they are in force for decades. In 1922 the Stormont Parliament in Belfast passed a Special Powers Act to be replaced only in 1973 by the Emergency Provisions Act passed by the Westminster Parliament in London. For over fifty years the government of Northern Ireland was empowered by emergency regulations to arrest without warrant, impose curfews, prohibit meetings and assemblies, employ administrative detention, prohibit the communication "by word of mouth" of rumors or incitements, and censor and prohibit the circulation of any newspaper, film, or recording not consonant with the "public interest." Under these powers, 4,434 Roman Catholics—4 per cent of the total Catholic population of Northern Ireland—were arrested without warrant between August 1971 and March 1972.[5]

The Republic of Ireland, which is governed by a democratic constitution, enacted an Offenses Against the State Act with the outbreak of war in Europe in 1939. This act standardized a number of emergency power statutes dating from 1922 that allowed for special criminal courts to insure "the effective administration of justice and the preservation of public peace and order" in times of emergency. From at least 1939 through 1972, the Irish government had the power to declare the ordinary courts inadequate and to set up special tribunals not bound to respect the full range of rights provided by the constitution. "Internment" or "preventive detention" could be ordered by a ministerial arrest warrant. The government increased the use of emergency powers as the civil strife in Northern Ireland increased and spilled over the border into the republic.

### Emergency Powers in the United States

Although the constitution of the United States has no specific emergency clause, the Congress is empowered to grant the President emergency powers in times of national crisis. In fact, beginning with the economic crisis of the 1930s, the various U.S. presidents have employed emergency powers for almost four decades in what a Senate special committee characterized as "virtually permanent states of emergency" that were terminated only in 1976.[6]

Of course, emergency powers once declared may be less than fully used, and most Americans were unaware that the powers were in force. But the U.S. government did use many of those powers during the Second World War. During that crisis, for example, American security agencies did not even purport to follow the usual rules of evidence when those rules might lead to the release of suspected spies or saboteurs. They made use of special administrative procedures for detaining suspect persons who could not have been convicted of crime under the protective rules of evidence. Administrative tribunals were used not only to detain but also to prosecute, convict, and execute suspected enemy agents.[7] Recourse to "preventive justice" is all but universal practice among democratic states in times of war or other national emergencies.[8]

The Japanese attack on Pearl Harbor prompted the military command of the Hawaiian Islands to declare martial law, the suspension of habeas corpus rights, the transfer of judicial powers from the civilian to the military courts, and the imposition of curfew regulations. Martial law was lifted only after the termination of hostilities.

Emergency powers were used to carry out the mass detention and relocation of Japanese aliens and Japanese-American citizens on the West Coast of the United States between 1942 and 1944. By executive order about 110,000 men, women, and children of Japanese origin were placed in detention centers, where they remained for the better part of the war. There was no evidence that any of them, individually or collectively, had conspired in, organized, or even contemplated subversive undertakings against the U.S. war effort. Elsewhere in the United States thousands of aliens from other enemy countries were detained for long periods of times solely at the discretion of the attorney general.

### Emergency Powers in Israel

Israel was founded amid the violence that followed World War II. At that time, the United Nations proposed a partitioning of Palestine—a proposal categorically rejected by the Arab states in the Middle East. A "War of Independence" (1948-49) followed, in which the Jews proclaimed the existence of Israel as a Jewish state. In the fragile peace that followed the Jews' successful defense of their new state, Israel was given provisional boundaries until a formal peace settlement could establish its permanent borders. Since the 1949 armistice, Israel has remained in a technical state of war with most of its Arab neighbors, with periodic explosions of hostilities like the "Six Day War" of 1967 and the "Yom Kippur War" of 1973. Throughout this extended period Israel's long and permeable borders have been penetrated by bands of Arab and non-Arab "irregulars" bent upon sabotage, attacks on civilian centers, reprisals, and the organization of popular "resistance." It has been under constant threat of attack.

Given this doleful history, it is not surprising that Israeli political life is characterized by the use of emergency powers. These powers have their legal basis in the Defense (Emergency) Regulations of 1945[9] promulgated by the British High Commissioner under the authority of the Palestine Defense Order-in-Council of 1937 to put down violence in the mandated territory. When the new Jewish administration assumed control over the new state in what had been part of the Palestine mandate, it assumed the powers of the British High Commissioner and the emergency powers of the 1945 Defense Regulations.

Those regulations provided for a comprehensive range of emergency powers, including the establishment of military courts (part II) to deal with designated "Military Court Offenses." Such offenses include possession and discharge of firearms and explosives (part III, arts. 58, 59) and interference with or damage to communications (art. 64), and the regulations apply to anyone who aids and abets in the commission of such acts, intends to commit such acts, or fails to reveal to the authorities the intention of others to commit such acts (arts. 65-67).

The regulations allow the security services not only to detain suspect persons but also to monitor and suppress "unlawful associations"—those that make "propaganda" and "incite" "hatred . . . contempt . . . or disaffection" toward, or acts of terrorism against, the duly constituted authority (part VII). Such proscriptions cover any person who is a member of, did any work or performed any service for, or attended a meeting of, any "unlawful association," or had in his possession "any book, account, periodical, handbill, poster, newspaper, or other document, or any funds, insignia, or property, belonging or relating to or issued by or in the interests of, or purporting to belong or relate to or be issued by or in the interests of, an unlawful association" (art. 85[f]). The regulations apply to all those who might "by writing, words, signs, or other acts of representation, directly or indirectly, whether by inference, suggestion, implication, or otherwise, act on behalf of, or as a representative of, an unlawful association" (art. 85[f]).

The censorship provisions of the regulations are very broad (part VIII). The censor can prohibit the publication of material "the publishing of which, in his opinion, would be, or be likely to be or become, prejudicial to the defense [of the nation] or to the public safety or to the public order" (art. 87). To these ends the censor is permitted to open and examine "all postal packets, and all printed or written matter and all packages, articles and things . . . which may contain any printed or written matter" (art. 89). The censor and his agents may subject travelers to search and interrogation (art. 92) and may confiscate any materials thought to be prejudicial to public safety and national defense.

The transfer of these emergency powers from the British High Commissioner to Israeli law in 1949 met with considerable resistance. During the British mandate period, some Jews had vociferously opposed the emergency regulations. A conference of lawyers in Tel Aviv in July 1946 held that the emergency regulations were in contravention of the "fundamental rights of men."[10] A few months after the state was established, Judge Shalom Kassan of an Israeli court sitting as the supreme court charged that the emergency laws "abolish the rights of the individual and, in particular, the control of the competent courts over the actions of authorities."[11] Nonetheless, the grave crisis faced by the fledgling state made it necessary to retain those regulations (with modifications) through the war of 1967 and to use them even more extensively in the occupation of the West Bank territories and Gaza after that war.[12]

The state of emergency declared four days after the establishment of the Israeli state still persists today.[13] Israel's democracy has been under emergency regulations for over three decades—its entire existence.[14]

The right of a sovereign state to preserve itself has always been acknowledged as basic to international law. During the deliberations that preceded the drafting of the Declaration on Rights and Duties of States by the U.N. International Law Commission in 1949, the right of a state to protect its survival was never questioned. In fact, the commissioners found it "tautological to say that an existing state has the right to exist; that right is in a sense a postulate or presupposition."[15]

From the moment of its birth, the state of Israel has faced a threat of extinction.[16] The vulnerability of its borders to "guerrilla" penetration,[17] the presence of a potentially subversive minority within its borders,[18] the quantitative military superiority of its opponents, and its demographic and industrial fragility have made emergency powers a functional necessity in Israel's effort to survive. Few Israelis are prepared to expose their state to a real threat of extinction in order to protect individual civil and political rights.

Given the circumstances, the emergency powers have been used with considerable discretion, and Israeli political life is surprisingly open. Information is freely available; even anti-government publications addressed specifically to the Arab population circulate freely. Arab publications must undergo prior censorship restrictions, and the control of Arab-language literature is fairly extensive, but in general the critical postures toward Israel expressed in Arab publications remain unimpaired. However, Arab political and labor organizations have suffered, within Israel itself and more particularly in the occupied territories of the West Bank and Gaza. Moreover, preventive detention of suspect Arabs is fairly common, and the Arabs' right of free assembly is often curtailed. These restrictions have brought upon Israel the censure of the U.N. General Assembly, Security Council, and Human Rights Commission.

The U.S. government too has voiced some serious concern about the limitations on civil and political rights in Israel, particularly those of Arab inhabitants of the occupied territories.[19] However, even the Carter administration with its focus on human rights could empathize with Israel in view of the complex problems it faced. And there is good reason to believe that with the reduction of tensions, the Israeli political system would restore the human rights characteristically made available by fully developed democratic states. Israel has the benefit of a long history of democratic thought. Most of the founders of Zionism came out of a European democratic tradition, and their commitments were, and are, democratic in inspiration and intention.

In a sense Israel at its founding was a "Third World" country—marked by some of the principal features of underdevelopment and burdened with the necessity of building a nation. It brought to these tasks of nation-building and rapid economic development a heritage of democratic-socialist convictions. That it took on the traits of an emergency regime in protracted crisis is the result of circumstances more than of deliberate policy.

Many less developed countries found themselves in somewhat similar circumstances two or three decades ago, when they began the ascent to modernity. Some, less democratic by conviction and less threatened by external factors, have lapsed into simple authoritarianism or have created non-competitive political systems. It has always been in the basic interest of the United States to encourage such countries to move toward democratic institutions as rapidly as possible. But effective influence requires a consistency and coherence not always found in U.S. foreign policy.

CHAPTER THREE

# Civil and Political Rights in the Republic of China

*The foundation of the government of the nation must be built upon the rights of the people. . . .*
SUN YAT-SEN[1]

THE NEW STATES THAT JOINED the international community in the wave of decolonization that followed the Second World War came from varied historical, cultural, and economic backgrounds. Many of them insisted that their newly attained sovereignty precluded even normal political influence from their former rulers or other outside sources. This demand often stemmed from a pervasive suspicion about the intentions of the former colonial powers, from a long experience with predatory "humanitarian interventions" that often brought oppression and humiliation in their train, or from a simple recognition that the new state was very fragile, and that the techniques thought necessary to insure its survival might not withstand international scrutiny.

Many a new state, duly armed at independence with a liberal constitution that may have been put together in some haste by the departing colonial power, very rapidly abandoned that constitution for another political form. Often the alternative chosen was a military dictatorship or a simple autocracy. Whatever the form, it had few features of what Western political scientists identify as "pluralistic" or "competitive" political systems.

Often these alternative political forms allow little if any competing political expression, little if any non-government-sponsored political activity. Political power is frequently monopolized by a "charismatic" ruler or a single party. If an election is held, it is generally a ritual of popular acclamation, not an opportunity to choose between alternatives.

Among the less developed countries (LDCs) there are also ideocratic political systems that have sacrificed civil and political rights, presumably in the service of their Marxist commitment to social and economic equality or their desire for rapid economic development. In many, such as Communist China, the economy is so deficient that the economic and social rights embodied in international covenants can be little more than rhetorical aspirations. Devoid of even a semblance of civil and political rights, their populations can anticipate little economic and social improvement without external assistance.

Today about half of the world's people live in political circumstances like these. About a third live in essentially open political systems—those that allow relatively free competition for public office and support that competition with explicit legal protections for such civil and political rights as free expression, free association, privacy, and due process.[2]

Almost all the competitive political systems are to be found among economies that are heavily industrialized and produce a relatively high per capita income. These countries, of which the United States is one, provide for substantially all the civil and political rights embodied in the International Covenant on Civil and Political Rights and most of the rights enshrined in the International Covenant on Economic, Social, and Cultural Rights. In such states there are legal rights weighted in favor of protecting the individual against his own government.

Between these extremes of open and closed societies, about 15 per cent of the world's people live in semi-competitive, more or less authoritarian regimes. Examples of such regimes are Senegal, Kenya, Bolivia, Egypt, Indonesia, Malaysia, Brazil, and Thailand. These countries suffer all the tensions of late or retarded economic development but have not yet opted for the constitutionally closed, non-competitive alternative that is so often attractive to LDCs.

Almost all remain non-Marxist, and frequently anti-Marxist, in political orientation.

Such regimes travel an unsteady course. In the face of tensions ranging from internal problems of population pressure, resource shortfall, threats of subversion, and pervasive illiteracy to external aggression, the temptation to insulate themselves in a constitutionally closed, non-competitive political environment is almost overwhelming. If traditional authoritarianism does not carry them there, there are always "Islamic Revolutionary Guards" or "People's Revolutionary Armies" waiting to accomplish the move.

But semi-competitive, authoritarian systems can sometimes make the transition to more open and competitive alternatives. Where it is still possible for interest groups to form and express themselves, the transition to competitive and pluralistic systems remains possible. Spain and Portugal provide evidence of that possibility.

It is in the interests of the United States—and it would be consonant with the human rights interests to which our political system has committed itself—to attempt, through foreign policy initiatives, to foster the movement of semi-competitive systems among the LDCs toward greater openness. Not only would these states be real or potential allies in situations where allies become strategic assets, but they would lend their voices to the international deliberations that will, in the future, give substance to a responsible characterization of "internationally recognized human rights." The example of the Republic of China on Taiwan (ROC) is instructive.

## THE EARLY YEARS ON TAIWAN

At the close of World War II, the ROC found itself in circumstances very much like those in which many other LDCs were subsequently to make their appearance. Confined to the island province of Taiwan and a few island fragments off the coast of continental China after the collapse of military resistance on the mainland, the ROC was burdened with all the disabilities of a newly decolonized LDC. Taiwan had been under Japanese colonial rule from 1895, when the treaty ending the Sino-Japanese war transferred the island from China to Japan, to the end of World War II, when it was returned to China. When the government of the Republic of China moved its seat to the city of Taipei in 1949, it inherited an island about 240 miles long and 90 miles at its widest. About the size of Massachusetts and Connecticut combined, the island had one of the highest population densities in the world, with an annual growth rate of about 3.5 per cent. More than half of its adult population was illiterate. The per capita annual income of approximately $175 was derived from agriculture, the main crops being sugar, pineapples, and rice. It had few mineral resources, and its marginal light industries had been badly damaged by Allied bombings during the closing years of the war.

As has happened to other LDCs on the occasion of decolonization, what had been "natural" trade relations were interrupted. Japan had been Taiwan's major, if not exclusive, trading partner; with the return of the island to China, trade with Japan was immediately severed. Taiwan's agricultural exports lost privileged access to the markets they had enjoyed for half a century.

The Japanese also withdrew all their administrative and technical personnel. Since the Taiwanese had not been trained in these functions, the control and technical infrastructure of the island suffered until the offices vacated by the Japanese could be filled by Nationalist Chinese immigrants fleeing the victorious Communist regime on the mainland.

Disorder was rampant on Taiwan at the end of World War II. The dispirited and defeated troops of the Nationalist government pillaged the island in a last effort to supply their beleaguered comrades still on the mainland. Corruption was a serious drain on whatever remained of the island's assets. The currency in circulation increased by an annual factor of about 750, and there was every evidence that the entire financial system would collapse. In February 1947, uprisings on the island were suppressed only with considerable violence.

By 1949 the Nationalist government had established control, but under very difficult conditions. Threatened by amphibious invasion from the Communist mainland, it was compelled to maintain a standing army of over half a million men. This military expense consumed about 60 per cent of the national budget and about 12 per cent of the island nation's gross national product.

Only the intercession of the United States in 1950 prevented a Communist military attempt to overwhelm the island. And it was only then that serious nation-building and economic reconstruction began. At that point, Taiwan faced the same problems as any number of other new states that came into being during the fifties and sixties.

But one major distinction was to have a significant influence on Taiwan's subsequent history. The government that transposed itself to the island after the Nationalist defeat had already been schooled by a generation of turbulent rule over much of mainland China. The transplanted "mainlanders" who were to preside over Taiwan's economic and political development had already suffered all the savage but instructive disappointments of revolution and military anarchy, armed national reunification, international war, and fratricidal civil war. They also brought with them an ideological heritage left them by Sun Yat-sen, founding father of the revolutionary republic that overthrew the dynastic system that had ruled China for thousands of years.

## The Legacy of Sun Yat-sen

Sun Yat-sen was one of those professional revolutionaries, so common to our times, who learned their political and revolutionary lessons from the advanced industrial states of the West in order to work revolution in their economically retarded homelands. As a political conspirator and revolutionary agitator, Sun was critically important in the revolution of 1911 that resulted in the abdication of the last Ch'ing emperor.

During his revolutionary apprenticeship, Sun put together an ideological system based on a nationalism that was a comprehensible reaction to imperialist penetration, a recognition that China required massive economic and industrial modernization, and a commitment to the parliamentary democracy he had come to know as an immigrant student in the American and British schools of Hawaii and Hong Kong.[3] On visits to his homeland while little more than a child, he had entertained his peers with tales of George Washington and the American struggle for independence.[4]

As a man, in 1904, Sun appealed to Americans for assistance, telling them that China's revolutionaries intended "to model [their] new government" after that of the United States.[5] Convinced that the U.S. constitution offered the best available guide, Sun in 1906 proposed a constitution for China that would include all the checks and balances of the American charter plus two others: an agency to supervise governmental technical competence through civil service examinations, and an institutional mechanism for the impeachment of officials found wanting. The proposed constitution would thus provide for the discharge of five powers: legislative, executive, judicial, examination, and control. The president of the republic would be elected by the sovereign people indirectly through a national assembly, which would consist of members directly elected by the people in their home districts and provinces.[6]

After the revolution that began in 1911 and deposed the imperial dynasty the following year, much of the Chinese political leadership was caught up in the effort to build viable political institutions for a nation wracked by pervasive illiteracy, oppressive poverty, political factionalism, and warlordism. The intellectuals around Sun Yat-sen, for their part, continued to advocate constitutional government modeled on the political systems of the West. By 1919 this advocacy had matured into a substantial body of literature. Sun had published his *Primer of Democracy* in 1917,[7] and the text of that work, subsequently identified as the "program for social reconstruction," became an integral part of the intellectual legacy left to his revolutionary heirs.

In one of the major theoretical journals of Sun's party, *Chienshe* [Reconstruction]—published in the years immediately before the death of Sun—the authors closest to him devoted an impressive amount of time and energy to analyses of the various representative systems available, and opted for forms of democracy that were among the most advanced in the world.[8] They translated texts that described experiments in more direct democracy—popular legislative initiative, referendum, and recall.[9]

By the time Sun Yat-sen put together his *San-min chu-i* [Three principles of the people], the final formulation of his political ideas,[10] he spoke of the ideal government as one informed by a "five-power constitution" that provided for the "four rights" of the people: popular sovereignty, the right to initiate legislation, the right to express collective judgments in referendums, and the right to recall elected officials by petition. Sun saw such a system as an effective defense against governmental malpractice and any threat to popular control.

After Sun's death in 1925, China lapsed into two decades of the turmoil characteristic of nations attempting to move from traditional to modern political and social arrangements. There were periods of near anarchy, military overlordship, protracted violence, war, invasion, and personal dictatorship. Only with the victory over Japan in 1945 was there an effort to put together a national constitution that might provide the legal basis for popular government.

## The Constitution of 1946

On December 25, 1946, a constitution was promulgated for the Republic of China. It provides for a democratic republic in which elected officials execute the will of the sovereign people (articles 1 and 2) and portrays the government as one that is "of the people, by the people, and for the people." The allusion to the words of Abraham Lincoln was a conscious effort to re-establish continuity with the ideas of Sun Yat-sen, who had regularly characterized his proposed government in Lincoln's formulation.[11] The intellectuals of Sun's early Kuomintang (Nationalist party) had regularly invoked that formula as well.[12]

The constitution of 1946 embodies the intentions of Sun Yat-sen. It provides equality and due process before a court required by law to be "non-partisan" (art. 80). It grants freedom of speech, association, assembly, religious and secular opinion, instruction, literary expression, publication, and residence, and also privacy of communications (art. 7-14). The rights to work, property, petition, suffrage, and access to public office are similarly guaranteed (art. 15-19).

The civil war between the forces of the Communist leader Mao Tse-tung and those of the central government was resumed before the constitution came into force. By the end of 1948 the military situation had deteriorated to the point that the central government was prepared to transfer to the island of Taiwan as a "final redoubt." The Nationalist government brought with it to Taiwan the remnants of the newly elected National Assembly and the Legislative Yuan (branch of government), as well as elements of the judiciary and the newly organized Examination Yuan and Control Yuan. It also brought its constitution.

## Proclamation of a State of Siege

Even before the move to Taiwan, however, the government had invoked the amendment clause of the constitution (art. 174[1]) to provide for the issuance of emergency regulations. On May 19, 1949, Taiwan and the small nearby islands still effectively controlled by the forces of the Nationalist government were placed under martial law. A general "state of siege" was proclaimed effective May 20.

"In order to secure public peace and order," the rights of individual citizens were greatly diminished. The proclamation of martial law imposed extensive curfew regulations, regulated commodity prices and controlled inventories, established security inspection requirements and personal identity procedures for travelers, and forbade the private possession of "arms, ammunition, or dangerous articles." Capital punishment was threatened for spreading rumors or for inciting fear, opposition to the government, or riots. Counterfeiting, using force during a robbery, committing arson, creating impediments to traffic, interfering with communications, disrupting water supplies, and damaging gas or electric facilities and services were all identified as capital crimes,[13] as were strikes by either workers or students.

The proclamation of a state of siege transferred civil administration and judicial matters to the control of military authorities. Military commanders were empowered to prosecute offenders, make disposition of private property, censor private and public communications, and control public assemblies.

In June 1949, a month after the proclamation of the state of siege, the Statute for Punishment of Rebellion was promulgated. It standardized the list of offenses subject to military intervention and prosecution. The statute identified all those offenses common to traditional criminal codes—such as the seizure of public lands, altering the constitution by illegal means, espionage, and conspiracy with a foreign power—but it also included provisions calculated to forestall the creation of a "climate of fear" that would be conducive to political violence and terrorism. Forbidden under these provisions were "participation in a rebellious organization or meeting" (art. 5), "circulating rumors or transmitting unfounded information to disturb public peace and order and beguile the population" (art. 6), and "making propaganda in favor of rebels by private communication, publication, or speech" (art. 7).[14]

In June 1950, a year after the proclamation of a state of siege, a Statute for Denunciation and Suppression of Rebels was promulgated. That statute included a provision for apprehending and punishing anyone who "knowingly fails to denounce rebels" (art. 9).[15]

Since 1950, the military authorities on Taiwan have had the responsibility of investigating, apprehending, and prosecuting persons charged with any of the above offenses. They can undertake administrative detention of such suspects; where evidence is insufficient for prosecution under court proceedings, such persons can be detained on order of the military commander for "security reasons." In effect, the widespread suspension of constitutionally guaranteed individual rights on Taiwan is based on some statutory regulations that in turn rest on emergency powers bestowed upon the president of the Republic of China by the National Assembly in 1948.

The ROC began its post-war history as a country animated by the democratic convictions of Sun Yat-sen and possessed of a democratic constitution. But the array of grave problems it faced fostered the creation of an emergency regime.

## CHAPTER FOUR

# The Protracted Crisis in the Republic of China

*Our situation is like that of a boat sailing through
rough seas. We can naturally ill afford to allow
unlawful elements to endanger our stability and
security. Consequently, we shall never pardon or
tolerate unlawful elements that engage in subversion
or other seditious activities.*

CHIANG CHING-KUO, 1978[1]

THE PRIME COMPONENT OF THE CRISIS in the Republic of
China is the massive military threat that has loomed over it since
the Communists took over the mainland. Technically, the ROC
remains at war with the Peking regime. Because of the ideological
nature of that war, there is also the threat of internal political
subversion.

While contending with the military threat, the authorities on
Taiwan have had to plan and administer a program of rapid economic and industrial development as complex and demanding as
any in the modern world. Such efforts generate tensions that have
destabilized many of the world's more favorably endowed developing countries.

A third element in the crisis was the simultaneous task of national integration and nation-building. When the Nationalist government transferred its seat to Taipei, it assumed control of a
Chinese population that, as a colony of Japan, had been separated
from the Chinese government for fifty years. As a consequence

there were cultural, linguistic, and political differences between the Chinese on Taiwan and the mainlanders who settled there, and these impeded national unity.

The external threat and the internal challenges of rapid economic development and nation-building added up to a grave and long-term crisis.

## THE MILITARY THREAT

With the collapse of Nationalist military resistance on the mainland, almost half a million men under arms—the remnants of the republican army—retreated to Taiwan as a "bastion." They were dispirited, malnourished, and afflicted with infectious diseases. Much of their heavy equipment had been abandoned, and support facilities on Taiwan and on the small offshore islands still held by the Nationalist forces were, at best, meager. By the end of the summer of 1949, the Chinese Communists had mobilized 300,000 troops opposite Taiwan to be sealifted in motorized junks and transports displacing in excess of 200,000 tons. What a Communist victory would mean was clear. After the military defeat of the Nationalists the Communist forces on the mainland began a campaign of extermination against the scattered remnants of the republican army and its "collaborators." By official Chinese Communist estimate, "1,830,000 Kuomintang reactionary troops and 980,000 bandit guerrilla forces" were "annihilated." Such violence continued for years, and as late as 1952 Mao Tse-tung himself officially announced that "there still remain more than 400,000 bandits scattered in remote areas to be annihilated." All "bandits, spies, local despots, and other counterrevolutionary elements . . . harmful to the people" were to be "resolutely eliminated."[2]

These were the circumstances that gave rise to the emergency regulations of May 1949 on Taiwan. The government had every reason to believe that an invasion by the Communist forces would culminate in massive blood-letting as well as the extinction of the Republic of China. Not only the republic itself but also a large minority of the population under its control was in mortal danger.

On January 5, 1950, President Harry Truman announced that the United States would not provide any further aid to the Nationalists to try to keep Taiwan from falling to the forces of Mao Tse-tung. In anticipation of that announcement, the Department of State had circulated a confidential memorandum to its information officers announcing the imminent fall of Taiwan.[3] Neither the United States nor the Communist forces on the mainland expected the Republic of China to resist the anticipated attack for very long. The situation was dramatically altered by the June 1950 invasion of South Korea by troops from the North. The United Nations declared the invasion "an act of aggression" and dispatched forces to aid South Korea. The United States bore the brunt of the fighting, and the Truman administration viewed the North Korean attack as part of a concerted effort by Communist nations to dominate Asia.

The United States put together a consortium of similarly disposed nations to resist, and because of its location and political support, Taiwan became a forward outpost on the defense perimeter of the "free world." Chinese Communist involvement in the Korean conflict intensified American strategic interest in Taiwan.[4] The American military saw the island as an "unsinkable aircraft carrier," critical to the defense of Asia and of great logistical value in any possible conflict on the continent. In May 1951, the United States dispatched a Military Assistance Advisory Group to Taiwan, positioned the Seventh Fleet to guard the Taiwan Strait (the 100-mile-wide channel between the island and the mainland), and stationed some American troops on the island as a tripwire to engage American forces in the event of an attack.

In December 1954 the U.S. secretary of state signed a mutual defense treaty between the United States and the ROC. This served as a significant deterrent to direct military attacks on Taiwan and its offshore islands. But only with the passage by the U.S. Congress early in 1955 of the Formosa (i.e., Taiwan) Resolution, which empowered the President to use U.S. forces against any attack on Taiwan "and such related positions and territories of that area now in friendly hands," did the Communist attacks on the offshore islands held by the ROC subside.

Then in August 1958 the People's Republic of China (PRC) began a massive bombardment of the offshore islands occupied by Nationalist forces. Over half a million artillery shells struck the islands, and the PRC set up a sea and air blockade to cut off supplies and communications to them. There were ten major air battles and four surface engagements between the air and naval units of the ROC and the PRC. Only the deployment of powerful United States air and naval forces into the area defused the situation.

By the mid-sixties, the dispute between the PRC and the Soviet Union had become both serious and public, and the PRC was compelled to abandon any immediate attempt at a military solution in the Taiwan Strait. By then the military force levels of the ROC had been significantly enhanced. As the seventies began it was clear that the PRC could launch an invasion of Taiwan only at a prohibitive cost and that the immediate military threat had been significantly reduced.

This did not mean either that the PRC had renounced the use of force to solve the "Taiwan issue" or that it was incapable of succeeding in such an enterprise should it choose to absorb the heavy manpower and materiel losses entailed. The official spokesmen of the Peking regime continued to insist that the "liberation" of Taiwan was an "internal" Chinese affair, and that while this "liberation" would be peaceful "so far as it is possible," force would be used "when all possibilities for peaceful negotiation have been exhausted or when peaceful negotiations have failed."[5]

During 1975 and 1976 the more militant members of the Chinese Communist hierarchy insisted that the Taiwan issue be resolved quickly by military force.[6] In July 1976, the naval, air, and ground forces of the PRC staged military maneuvers in which air and naval units went farther into the Taiwan Strait than ever before. In the negotiations that led to the recognition of the PRC by the Carter administration, the PRC refused to renounce the use of force in the Taiwan area, continuing to insist that the "liberation" of Taiwan was an internal Chinese affair and that any such renunciation would infringe upon the sovereign initiatives of the People's Republic of China.

Since 1960, the PRC has built the largest army and the third-largest air force and navy in the world. Its defense budget is exceeded only by those of the United States and the Soviet Union. It has almost a 10-1 superiority over the ROC in personnel and is superior in most categories of major military equipment. In 1981 the Chinese Communists had about 4.75 million men under arms in regular units plus approximately 7 million members in local militia, suitable only for defense use. Their navy of some 2,650 vessels included about 15 destroyers armed with surface-to-surface Styx-type missiles (SSMs); 17 frigates, at least half of which are similarly armed; over 100 fully armed attack submarines; about 195 multi-mission fast attack craft armed with SSMs; 230 motorized torpedo boats; and more than 100 armed hydrofoils. The PRC air force numbers about 400,000 men and 5,000 to 6,000 combat aircraft.

Across the Taiwan Strait, the ROC maintains about half a million men under arms. Its navy has about 340 combatant units, including 22 over-age destroyers, only 5 or 6 of which are armed with SSMs; 2 unarmed submarines; 11 lightly armed frigates; and perhaps 10 to 20 fast attack craft, a few of which are armed with SSMs. The two unarmed submarines are for training purposes; the ROC has ordered from Holland two armed (though obsolescent) submarines.[7]

While Taiwan enjoys the strategic advantage of 100 miles of blue water between itself and its potential adversary, the disparity in force levels is oppressive. The economy of Taiwan is almost totally dependent on foreign trade. The PRC has the capability to deploy a naval blockade that could strangle the ROC into submission, if the PRC were willing to pay the political costs of interfering with the commerce of Taiwan's trading partners, notably the United States and Japan.[8] When the nuclear arsenal available to the Chinese Communist forces is considered as well, the picture becomes quite ominous.

The leadership in Peking has shown itself disposed to embark on military adventure when it decides its "national interests" are at stake. In February 1979, just two months after it had been officially recognized by the United States, Peking invaded the Socialist

Republic of Vietnam (SRV). This was an undertaking that many American analysts had dismissed as too perilous to consider. The SRV had just signed a friendship treaty with the Soviet Union—which had massive military forces deployed along the northern and western borders of the PRC. Nonetheless, the PRC engaged about twenty infantry and six armored divisions, supported by a thousand combat aircraft, in a "punitive war" against Vietnam.[9] The PRC proved itself prepared to risk a major conflict with the Soviet Union in order to evidence its strength in defending its "national interests."

The leadership of the ROC can therefore take little comfort in the assessment of some American strategists that the PRC would not attack Taiwan for fear of alienating the United States or Japan. The government in Peking has shown that it is willing to undertake the most dangerous of adventures to serve some ill-defined national purpose, or to achieve some obscure gains.

The ROC, then, has for over thirty years faced a committed opponent with enormous military capabilities. The military threat alone would seem to warrant the continuance of the emergency regulations invoked in 1948 and 1949. But there is also another aspect to the threat.

## THE THREAT OF SUBVERSION

Almost since its inception, theoretical Marxism has been preoccupied with the various forms of irregular warfare and subversion as revolutionary instruments. Friedrich Engels wrote extensively on the role of "people's" or "guerrilla" warfare in the course of revolution.[10] Both he and Karl Marx devoted considerable time and intellectual energy to devising a strategy of popular revolutionary mobilization that would make use of violence and terror. By Lenin's time, the tactics of revolutionary subversion had been reasonably well worked out. Mao Tse-tung was schooled in these tactics, and by the time of the Communist victory on the mainland, he had put together a well-rounded program of political infiltration, subversion, mass violence, terrorism, and military assault.

## Stage One: A "United Front"

The strategy of subversion involves a disposition to be conciliatory at first, to negotiate and compromise, as long as one's opponent has the advantage in numbers or position. Lenin had advocated such a policy as early as 1920.[11] Compromise, negotiation, and flexibility, together with an effort to piece together a "united front" against any determined enemy, are the tactics of the first stage. There are attempts to collaborate with any elements that might be of service in undermining the strength and stability of those identified as principal opponents.

The "united front against fascism" used by Communists in Europe during the interwar years is an application of this tactic. Since "fascism" was then the principal target, tactical collaboration could be undertaken with the representatives of social and liberal democracies.[12] "Bourgeois democratic" instrumentalities could be used to defeat the "fascist bourgeois dictatorship." After the defeat of the principal antagonist, fascism, the Communists could then initiate a program that would ensure the success of Communist revolution and the advent of the "dictatorship of the proletariat."

## More Demands; Violence and Terror

Organization of a "people's" or "popular" front was to provide the opportunity for Communists to infiltrate and dominate non-Communist organizations that opposed the government for one reason or another and whose opposition could be exploited by trained revolutionary professionals.[13] As crises deepened, Communist revolutionaries could influence such organizations to raise their demands and provoke violence in order to draw the government into an ever-tightening cycle of reaction. At that point, Marx himself had said as early as 1848, there was "only *one means* by which the murderous death agonies of the old society and the bloody birth throes of the new society can be *shortened,* simplified, and concentrated—and that is by *revolutionary terror.*"[14]

While Engels scathingly rejected terrorist tactics that were used indiscriminately,[15] he was equally emphatic that given a situation of protracted crisis, an effectively organized "handful of people," providing "one small push" with terrorist violence, might succeed in overthrowing a system. Both Marx and Engels argued that the use of violence and terror could be successful only at the conjunction of political and socioeconomic crises.[16]

Lenin's arguments were very similar. Violence and terror were "subordinate" and auxiliary tactics to be employed only after the infiltration of "popular" organizations by committed Communist agents. Only then, and in suitable circumstances, could assassination of selected individuals such as members of the constabulary and the military, the theft of property, and armed attacks on "police spies" be undertaken. At that point terrorism could be used against "brutal government officials" to revolutionary purpose.[17] Lenin admonished his followers:

> Go to the youth. Organize at once, and everywhere, fighting brigades among students, and particularly among workers. Let them arm themselves immediately with whatever weapons they can obtain—rifles, revolvers, bombs, knives, brass knuckles, clubs, rags soaked in kerosene to start fires with, rope or rope ladders, shovels for building barricades, dynamite cartridges, barbed wire. . . Some can undertake to assassinate a spy or blow up a police station, others can attack a bank to expropriate funds for an insurrection. Let every squad learn, if only by beating up police.[18]

The initial phase of the strategy of subversion is almost indistinguishable from any other political enterprise. It involves participation in local interest groups, each pursuing its own parochial concerns. Only when a political system is involved in protracted crisis does the infiltration of revolutionary agents begin to pose a special problem.

Conspiratorial revolutionary groups discipline themselves under principles of "democratic centralism," a form of party control that makes individuals the carriers of an organized program of subversion. From that base, revolutionary agents infiltrate interest groups with the clear intention of "isolating" any "reactionary" elements within them that might obstruct the agents' purposes. "Progressive" elements are fostered, and gradually the non-revolutionary group takes on more and more revolutionary features. Democracy is used, in effect, to orchestrate the forces that will ultimately be used to subvert it.[19]

After the "masses" have been organized in such a fashion, under the direct or indirect tutelage of the revolutionary party—and after the necessary combination of economic and political crises has matured—it becomes, in the words of Mao Tse-tung, "necessary to create terror for a while."[20] The consequence is that the "popular front" very rapidly transforms itself into a militant revolutionary agency for the destruction of the established authority.

This entire strategy—united-front tactics in which non-Communist organizations were shaped to revolutionary purposes, the intensifying of demands with the onset of crisis, the introduction of violence and terror, and finally, direct military confrontation when the forces of "reaction" had been sufficiently weakened and disorganized—was the strategy used with great success by Mao Tse-tung on the Chinese mainland.[21] Having already experienced this strategy and its disastrous results, the Nationalists would have shown monumental stupidity had they failed to anticipate and impede an attempt to carry it out on Taiwan.

## The February 28 Incident

At the time of the declaration of a "state of siege" in 1949, the Nationalist government on Taiwan enjoyed little legitimacy. It had regained control of the island only four years before, when the island was returned to China after World War II. And in February 1947, the island had exploded in armed rebellion—the "*Erh Erh Pa* (February 28, 1947) Incident."

The rebellion was precipitated by local conditions. The first of the Nationalist Chinese administrators sent to the island, Governor-General Chen Yi, was by and large incompetent, corrupt, and brutal.[22] He brought with him disorderly troops, and proceeded to deplete the island's assets by wide-scale confiscations purportedly to supply the Nationalist resistance on the mainland. During the Second World War, agricultural production on the island had fallen to about half the 1937 level, and by 1945 food was in very short supply. As a consequence, commodity prices in January 1947 had risen about 700 per cent for food, 1,400 per cent for fuel and construction materials, and 25,000 per cent for agricultural fertilizer.[23]

These conditions would have been enough to generate massive unrest. But it is clear that some Communist agents and Communist sympathizers were involved in the organization of violence. On February 1, 1947, four weeks before the outbreak of mass violence, Mao Tse-tung had called for a "new high tide of the Chinese revolution."[24] Riots and student rebellions were to be used to undermine the remaining resistance of the Kuomintang, the Nationalist party.

When the rebellion of February 1947 was suppressed, many Communist agents and non-Communist dissidents fled the island to become immediately active in the Chinese Communist party on the mainland. There they recruited and trained agents to assume administrative posts on Taiwan after "liberation."

Since that time, as though to confirm their influence, the Chinese Communists have claimed responsibility for the February 1947 rebellion and have annually convened meetings to honor the event. Those meetings are characterized by the "popular front" format long employed by Communists to enlist opponents of the Nationalists, whatever their particular persuasion, in the service of Marxist revolution. Participants have included members of the Taiwanese "Democratic Self-Government League," Taiwanese members of the People's Congress Standing Committees, former Kuomintang generals, some of the known defectors from Taiwan, and persons who as professors, students, and activists had taken part in the February 1947 uprising.[25]

## THE ECONOMIC CHALLENGE

Despite a grave external threat and considerable evidence of organized internal subversion, the Republic of China on Taiwan was compelled to embark upon a highly ambitious program of economic development. The shattered economy had to be rebuilt if the island were to support its pre-1949 population and the large numbers of newly arrived mainlanders, both military and civilian. Furthermore, the military establishment required an industrial base. Finally, the political leadership had brought with it the social and economic programs of Sun Yat-sen, which called for rapid economic development and industrialization. All these considerations required the newly established government to undertake strenuous—and inevitably destabilizing—economic changes.

And so the population of Taiwan suddenly found itself thrust into an unfamiliar and non-traditional social, economic, and political environment. There was a massive redistribution of assets through a systematic land reform program headed by General Chen Cheng, who was one of Chiang Kai-shek's most important military commanders and later, until his death in 1965, Chiang's political heir-apparent.[26] First the rent on share-cropped land was reduced to a maximum of 37.5 per cent of the total annual yield of agricultural main crops. By May 1949, 302,000 farm families had entered into new leases governed by the rent-reduction legislation. Almost a third of all arable land was involved in the program, and over 40 per cent of all farm households were affected.

Almost immediately thereafter the "land-to-the-tillers" program was instituted. Landlords were forced to sell any land in excess of 7.16 acres to those who actually worked the soil, and over 170,000 acres were sold. By 1953 about one-fourth of the cultivated acreage of Taiwan had changed hands. This was done without violence. But since the actual value of the land is estimated to have been about 4 to 6 times the land's annual yield and the compensation to the landlords was only about 2.5 times that yield, much of the land-owning class was left with grievances, while the much more numerous tenant class benefited.

These reforms helped fuel the first phase of the economic development of Taiwan,[27] one of the best managed programs of modernization in the contemporary world. Between 1950 and 1970, the island had a higher overall rate of growth and greater family income equity than all other East Asian countries except Japan.[28]

But these rapid changes in the island's economy created very volatile political conditions. Land-holders resented having to sell part of their land and to sell it at less than full value. Peasants were confused and disoriented by the waves of change. As industrialization took hold, the development of an urban and semi-urban work force introduced new tensions. At the same time, hundreds of thousands of immigrants from the mainland fed the programs of modernization with their technical, professional, and administrative skills by occupying positions previously held by the Japanese. All this generated social tension that opened opportunities for political infiltration and subversion.

In addition, a latent "ethnic" problem threatened to act as a catalyst for other sources of discontent. Since the suppression of the rebellion of 1947 there had remained a "mainlander-Taiwanese" tension that at first was very corrosive. This tension was fueled by the real and fancied privileges that the Taiwanese saw among the mainlander immigrants. Many of the mainlanders had served in the military and were supported by welfare benefits and readjustment preferences. Others came to Taiwan with education and skills largely absent from the resident population. There were also historical and cultural differences plus a language difference: the mainlanders spoke Mandarin and most Taiwanese spoke their own dialect of Fukienese. All this created the potential for division and tension.

The multiple threats to the survival of the Republic of China on Taiwan, and the violence and human suffering that would predictably attend the nation's dissolution, provide a *prima facie* rationale for emergency constraints. Nonetheless, those limitations on civil and political rights have been used with considerable restraint, and the scope of military jurisdiction has been gradually reduced. According to the 1952 "Measure Governing the Classification of Cases to Be Tried by the Military Judicial Organ. . ." as subsequently amended, civilians are now subject to a military trial only if they commit one of three types of crimes: sedition and espionage; theft or unauthorized sale or purchase of military equipment and supplies; or theft or damage of public communications equipment and facilities.[29] In the late seventies, however, the government temporarily extended the use of military trials to try to stem the rapid increase in homicides and robberies.

As the Republic of China entered the decade of the seventies, the emergency regime had survived twenty years of crisis without massive violence, population expulsion, mass murder, or whole-sale arrests. Tight controls had maintained stability and continuity under conditions that had precipitated political collapse in many other parts of the less developed world.

## NEW CHALLENGES: THE WEST AND PEKING

During the seventies, however, the ROC was to face yet another series of challenges, marked by serious diplomatic reverses. The challenges began with a dispute with Japan over the sovereignty of a group of small, barren islands off Okinawa. The United States supported Japan's claims to the islands that both the mainland Chinese and the Chinese of Taiwan had long held to be their own. At almost the same time, President Richard Nixon began his overtures toward the "normalization" of relations with the government in Peking. The PRC had long since made known its preconditions for normalization. They included the withdrawal of recognition of the Republic of China, abrogation of the mutual defense treaty between that nation and the United States, and a complete withdrawal of all American military personnel from Taiwan. This would mean that the Republic of China not only would be divested of the recognition of its legitimacy by a nation it considered its most faithful ally but also would lose that ally's military deterrent support.

The Nixon initiatives caused an immediate erosion of support for the ROC in the United Nations. More and more countries chose to recognize the mainland regime and to withdraw recognition of the ROC. By September 1972 even the Japanese, long associated with the Republic of China as both friend and ally, had withdrawn diplomatic recognition.

### The Ferment for Reform

Those defeats promoted a discontent on Taiwan that began to take on some of the features of political upheaval. Soon the criticisms began to focus not only on the diplomatic failures of the regime but on its domestic behavior as well. By 1971 a significant minority of intellectuals, students, and professors from the most prestigious institutions had already begun a wide-ranging discussion of the nation's future course. They gathered around the journal *Ta-hsueh tsa-chih* [The intellectual] to advance reform proposals that contained substantial criticism of government policy. Between 1971 and 1973 the criticism was free-wheeling, often impressively appropriate, at times carping, but almost always conducted with evident concern and patriotic resolve.[30]

Academics and students spoke of the lack of openness in the intellectual and political processes—the pervasive sense that those who were prepared to speak out were always subject to "surveillance." They poignantly urged the government to allow educated youth and professional academics to contribute more freely and effectively to the political deliberations that would determine the nation's future. They advocated rejuvenation of the political elite by means of more ready access to the centers of power for "young men of talent." They appealed to the rule of public law to reduce corruption and arbitrary actions, and they championed a more open society animated by pluralistic values.

The reformist intellectuals were anti-Communist in inspiration, and the regime on the mainland was the antithesis of the society to which they aspired. Their concerns were for increased democracy and an expanding and equitable economy in a secure and stable community. In October 1971, fifteen intellectuals prepared a manifesto that contained essentially these proposals. The signatories included Professors Chen Ku-ying, Yang Kuo-shu, Su Chun-hsiang, and Sun Chen of National Taiwan University, and Professors Chiu Hungdah and Lu Chun-pu of National Chengchi University. Central to their concerns was the expansion of civil and political rights that had been curtailed for two decades by the emergency regulations.

Beyond that, some of the criticism began to be addressed to the basic accomplishments of the regime. Students and some faculty insisted that unjustifiable inequities had marred the developmental process, and that the system exploited the workers and the peasants for the advantage of monied interests. The discussions began to take on a suspiciously Marxist flavor. In 1973 two professors, Chen Ku-ying and Wang Shao-po, were arrested by military authorities when it was revealed that they had participated in seminars in Berkeley, considered a center of radical views in the United States, and had brought to Taiwan tapes of speeches made by visitors to the People's Republic of China. In the spring of 1974, Professor Sun Chih-yen, chairman of the philosophy department at National Taiwan University, charged that some members of his faculty were propagating Chinese Communist thought and working directly or indirectly to subvert the social and political system on Taiwan.

## The Government Response

Throughout the entire period in which the ferment for reform agitated the Taiwan intellectuals, the government made its position transparently clear through a series of conferences and publications. The Kuomintang party organ, *Chung-yang jih-pao* [Central daily], published an extended critique of some aspects of the reform movement.[31] The long article, carefully crafted, was given wide circulation and clearly expressed the official position on the prospects of political reform.

The chief argument made by the government spokesmen was that the ROC was in a protracted crisis and that any reforms would have to be undertaken with a prudent regard for stability. Student preoccupation with the future of the nation could, in principle, contribute to national well-being. The danger was that legitimate student and intellectual concern might be exploited to serve other purposes. Pointed references were made to the destabilizing impact of the student movement in France, which for a time seemed to threaten the very integrity of the French state. France, the argument proceeded, was in a position to allow subversive and destabilizing student dissent, but the Republic of China on Taiwan was not. The criticism of intellectuals would have to be well calculated so that it could not be used to mobilize subversive sentiment.

In the circumstances in which the Republic of China finds itself, the term "subversive" has an extended meaning. At least two developments could precipitate action against Taiwan by Peking. One is any effort to declare Taiwan sovereign and independent of any connection with the mainland. The Peking government has regularly insisted that any such effort would not be tolerated. As a consequence, any effort to put together a Taiwan "independence movement" has been rigorously suppressed. The second circumstance that might well set off a catastrophic chain of events would be large-scale political and social disturbances on the island. The PRC has always maintained that Taiwan is an integral part of the "one China," and so any large-scale violence might call forth Chinese Communist intervention in what they would regard as "domestic" disorder.

For these reasons the government in Taipei has always been very firm with the spokesmen of radical reforms. In the early seventies it advised intellectuals to proceed with caution in their criticism so as not to be drawn into providing a rationale for "Taiwanese independence," public unrest, violence, or the establishment of a "popular front" to begin the process of revolutionary change sought by the ROC's opponents across the Taiwan Strait.

An example of what the government took to be a lack of caution and an impaired sense of responsibility was the "social science inquiries" that some student groups embarked upon during this period. Students organized "social science teams" that fanned out into the general society and put together "findings" after two days of orientation and ten days of "field work" in seventy-two townships and villages. What resulted were some very colorful, sometimes tragic, impressionistic accounts of poverty, exploitation, alienation, and hopelessness.

The government response was to ask some prominent economists and social scientists to participate in a forum sponsored by the journal Ta-hsueh tsa-chih [The intellectual]. These scientists calmly catalogued the methodological shortcomings of such "studies," which did not have adequate sampling procedures, controls for subjective judgment, or a statistical base for assessing the measures of family income. The language of the student "studies" had been emotional rather than analytical, and the use of a single "demonstrative case" to generalize about conditions of whole classes fell short of sound scientific inquiry.

The evidence was, in fact, that Taiwan in its developmental history was characterized by a higher degree of family-income equality than any other developing nation in the world.[32] Unlike almost all other developing countries, Taiwan did not buy economic and industrial modernization by increasing income disparities.

Taiwan had not suffered the disruptive trade-off between growth and equity that most Western economists thought was inevitable for countries undergoing rapid modernization and industrialization. Furthermore, its rate of unemployment was not high by relevant standards of comparison.[33] Finally, the fact that some capitalists on Taiwan realized substantial profits in their enterprise was the necessary consequence of the choice of a non-command form of economic growth. Unless the Republic of China were to espouse a centralized, bureaucratized, thoroughly nationalized economy, it had to have the capitalist accumulation of profit for investment and to reward risk-taking and offset depreciation.

The general thrust of the official position was that unless one accepted the Marxist definition of "exploitation"—that everyone who works for wages is by definition exploited, simply because he is not worth his hire unless his labor contributes to a return on the owners' investment—the student criticism of the system was unwarranted and irresponsible. More than that, it provided the language and the rationale for dissident movements and a ground for Communist infiltration.

For the authorities on Taiwan these were vital issues. Such "studies" and systemic criticism could not be seen as innocent intellectual exchanges. Under the ominous threat of Communist military intervention from across the Taiwan Strait and Communist subversion from within, any intellectual dissidence that took on the flavor of a Marxist critique of the mixed economy of the Republic of China, and provided the moral justification for mass unrest, posed a serious threat. It was a criticism directed at the very foundations of the system. It challenged two decades of accomplishments, made in the face of great adversity, and it tended to question the legitimacy of the system and alienate allegiance.

Through public counterargument, oblique threat, and relatively mild suppression (some professors were fired; some were relieved of their teaching posts and assigned research tasks), the government defused the more extreme criticism. At the same time, efforts were made to introduce both substantial and symbolic reforms. In May 1972, when Chiang Ching-kuo, the son of Chiang Kai-shek, became premier, he committed himself to providing a more democratic and freer way of life for the Chinese on Taiwan—a way of life that could serve as an alternative to that under which the population of mainland China labored.

## Reforms Under Chiang Ching-kuo

As part of this enterprise, Chiang Ching-kuo very rapidly brought a respectable number of native-born Taiwanese into the highest echelons of government. He recruited into government service many American-trained young men—the "young men of talent" of whom the reformists had spoken. New procedures for public petition to the Executive Yuan (branch) were implemented. Individuals who thought their rights had been violated could express their grievances directly; responses were generally to be made within thirty days, with longer periods provided for more complex cases. In all cases the petitioner was to be kept informed of the resolution of his complaint. Measures were adopted to control corruption in government and wasteful expenditure. Even members of the Taiwan Garrison Command—the military unit charged with enforcing martial law—were not exempt, and in 1972 some relatively high-ranking members of the command were convicted in connection with smuggling. Wang Cheng-yi, chief of the Personnel Administration Bureau of the Executive Yuan, was prosecuted for accepting bribes in connection with construction projects. Even though he was a relative of Chiang Ching-kuo himself, Wang was sentenced to life imprisonment.

Plans were made for a system of social welfare and health benefits for the working population. A new labor law provided for reorganization of the Chinese Federation of Labor; in principle, the law allowed workers the right to strike, but strike activity has been almost unknown on Taiwan. Extensive programs of rural redevelopment were introduced, and price supports were proposed for agricultural producers. Heavy investments were budgeted for expansion of the support infrastructure for the rural economy. An effort was made to increase the decentralization of industry so that rural workers could have access to industrial wages.

Finally, Chiang Ching-kuo undertook a direct personal campaign to bring the government to the people. He addressed youth groups, visited rural areas, and vowed to create an "honest, efficient, and capable government."[34]

In effect, by the mid-seventies, the government on Taiwan was attempting to satisfy what were understood to be "responsible" demands for reform. Civil and political rights were warily extended. Each extension was closely assessed in terms of its potential threat to the security of a political system deeply embroiled in crisis. As a case in point, for years the Taipei government has allowed free emigration (though with some notable exceptions) and permitted students to leave Taiwan for study—primarily in the United States—with full knowledge that as many as 90 per cent might succumb to the lure of job opportunities, the possibility of upward mobility, more ample opportunities for self-expression, and other benefits in the United States and Europe. The loss of talent through such a drain was considered acceptable. Such expatriates might well return some day when the island offered them greater opportunities. More than that, permitting the right to leave was consonant with the style of a mixed economy with elaborate international connections. And finally, intellectuals who were not allowed the right to pursue the best education available anywhere in the world would constitute a potential resource for disaffection.

Similarly, the right of free expression was gradually extended because it was recognized that the extension would help relieve frustration and reduce the potential for bitter resistance. Criticism flourished as long as it did not begin to take on the features of systemic and radical rejection. But any evidence of flirtation with Marxist ideologies, any contact with representatives of the mainland regime or participation in pro-Communist activities, could lead to "Communist front" tactics that in Taiwan's crisis circumstances might bring on a cycle of dissent, suppression, and more enflamed resistance. The officials on Taiwan remain convinced that once such a process is begun, it can be halted only with a severe strain that could have regrettable consequences. There are always external forces prepared to insinuate themselves into the process and provide it with massive support.

The Chinese on Taiwan have had enough experience with political violence to recognize the threat of subversion and terrorism.[35] If this possibility is granted, a number of considerations follow. American social science literature that is respected by intellectuals influential among Taiwan's political leadership holds that a political community faced with the threat of internal and external subversion, perhaps involving violence and terror, should undertake preemptive "intelligence and contingency planning." It should employ "more stringent customs procedures" and maintain enhanced "security at embassies and airports." It should develop and circulate "screening profiles to identify terrorists" and subversives, and organize "clandestine counter-terrorist organizations. . . ."[36] Moreover, since "the main source of strength of . . . terrorism is publicity," threatened regimes are advised to maintain wary control of the press.[37] Only by severing the link between the potential revolutionary and his media audience can the effectiveness of "popular front" tactics that begin with something like "radical reform" and conclude with revolutionary terrorism be significantly curtailed.[38]

While accepting such counsel, which, if rigorously pursued, would seriously jeopardize civil and political freedoms, ROC authorities have also shown a willingness to reduce the weight of such restrictions when they could do so without increasing the threat to the community. Clearly such a strategy renders authoritarian rule much more tolerable and favors stability and continuity. It allows discontent to dissipate before pressures can mount to impair the system.

For the population, such a policy allows the relatively free flow of information and a substantial measure of civil and political rights. On Taiwan there is free access to a variety of news sources. Standard American news publications, for example, are available; *Time* and *Newsweek* are easily obtainable in urban areas and in most major libraries. The public radio and television broadcasting systems offer a varied fare with self-censorship the standard control mechanism used. There is some restraint on books from foreign sources, but those restraints fall almost exclusively on Marxist literature or what is perceived as "Marxist" by some vague set of criteria. There is public talk of the ubiquity of "agents of the security service," but as almost anyone who has been in Taipei for any length of time knows, such allusions do little to dampen the ardor of public political discussion. Arrests without warrant and searches without judicial permission are now relatively rare. There is an occasional charge of police brutality, but documented cases are now almost impossible to find.

## "Sedition" in the ROC

The official figures made available in 1978 claim that only 254 persons convicted of "sedition" by military tribunals are serving sentences on Taiwan, and that only one person was put to death for that offense. When Amnesty International published its assessment of political and civil liberties on Taiwan in 1980, it estimated that anywhere from 400 to "several thousand" persons were in prison there for expressions of "political dissidence." In 1976, Amnesty International had announced that it had the names of approximately 200 persons so incarcerated.[39]

Resolving such discrepancies is no easy matter. An estimate that ranges as widely as that of Amnesty International is intrinsically suspect. Moreover, Amnesty International counts as "prisoners of conscience" many who have simply suffered detention as well as many who were convicted of offenses other than "sedition." But the official government figures cannot be subjected to independent corroboration.

"Sedition" as defined in the Republic of China on Taiwan refers to acts that support "with action the Chinese Communist totalitarian regime, including participation in subversion, instigation of violence, and the spying out of national secrets for Communist agents."[40] This broad definition includes those acts stipulated in the Statute for Punishment of Rebellion and the Statute for Denunciation and Suppression of Rebels—participating in a rebellious organization or meeting, making propaganda in favor of rebels in correspondence, publications, or public addresses, or failing to denounce those suspected or guilty of such offenses.

The laws governing subversion, sedition, engaging in political incitement, or creating a climate conducive to political violence are therefore much broader in scope on Taiwan than would be tolerated in a Western democracy in *normal* times. Moreover, infractions of these laws are handled by military authorities, who—no matter how constrained and public the procedures—can be expected to deal with offenders in a more summary fashion than the civilian courts and to mete out more severe penalties.

Once again, these limitations on human rights must be assessed in context. The ROC authorities see the organization of opposition as the first phase of a well-established process of revolutionary subversion. As they understand the process, its first phase involves the establishment of a "democratic reform" opposition that gradually expands into anti-government "popular front" activities. That phase, given the tensions that attend rapid social and economic change, diplomatic isolation, fossil fuel shortfall, or any number of other conceivable dislocations, might easily escalate into widespread unrest. During this stage there is agitation for more liberties and a reduction of security surveillance. The attempt is made to put together an organizational infrastructure that could gather tactically useful information and identify individuals, groups, and resources that might provide collateral support in any subsequent phase.

The next stage involves an attempt to expand propaganda and agitation. Legal or clandestine measures are taken to establish a political party or, barring that, suitable front groups that organize protest marches, strikes, and petitions, and may provoke episodic violence.

The final stage—systematic violence and terrorism—is expected to occur in conjunction with indirect support or overt military intervention by the PRC.[41] The general conviction among the authorities on Taiwan is that if the process is not aborted before the more advanced stages of insurgency, it can be halted only with great difficulty, if at all.[42]

Over the years, as the abatement of tensions permitted, the management of public affairs has increasingly been returned to civilian authorities, and the restrictions on the general population have been significantly reduced. Today, in Taiwan, constitutionally legitimized civilian agencies handle nearly all public matters, and the great majority of the citizens have no occasion to encounter the emergency regulations. Clearly, the existence of the regulations perpetuates an uncomfortable level of anxiety among the citizens. But no substantial group of citizens on Taiwan, no matter how disaffected by circumstances, appears to favor allowing the island to fall under mainland Communist domination.[43] To avoid that fate the citizens are apparently prepared to suffer a limitation on traditional democratic liberties. The trade-off was expressed by a leading non-Kuomintang Taiwanese politician in 1976: "Right now Taiwan's survival is more important to the people than whether it has more or less democracy."[44]

## CHAPTER FIVE

# The Political Culture of the Republic of China

*To Dr. Sun will have to go the credit of having made the revolution an effective force and of having crystallized public opinion behind a democratic movement, which has survived all the mistakes and the reactions of the past . . . years. . . . We shall forget everything about him but one outstanding fact and that is that he was the champion of democracy in China. . . . Only the large fact of his life will remain, his struggle against despotism, his struggle against corruption, his struggle for the right of the governed to a say in the government. And throughout the country his thought sweeps the minds of the people. . . . As men speak it and write it and read it, a spirit will be abroad in the land which will make itself felt. . . .*

T'ANG SHAO-YI, 1925[1]

To ASSESS THE LEVEL OF HUMAN RIGHTS in a state, one must be acquainted with the operating political culture within which these rights are granted or denied. To speak very generally, a "political culture" is composed of what the people who live under a particular system have learned to accept and expect from that system. Those expectations are informed by an amalgam of traditional culture, inherited opinion, and current ideology—shaped by external pressures as well as by recent internal political experience.

What should be of concern to all Americans as citizens of a democratic state in a relatively hostile world environment, and especially to U.S. policy-makers charged with sustaining that democracy and furthering its long-term interests, is whether an evolving political culture displays support for movement toward freer institutions or toward non-competitive forms of political rule.

## Democratic Influences in the ROC

Long before the Republic of China was established on Taiwan, the political thought of Sun Yat-sen had become the official ideology of the Kuomintang (KMT), the Nationalist party. As a consequence, democratic aspirations had become part of the common political language among the Chinese. Since the Nationalist move to Taiwan, the elements of political democracy have become an irrepressible part of the thought pattern of the majority of the Chinese on the island. Most Taiwanese were born after the Nationalists came to Taiwan and have been systematically schooled in the rhetoric, if not the subtlety, of Sun Yat-sen's *San-min chu-i*. Both the justifications and the criticisms of the current political system on Taiwan, in fact, are couched in the terminology of liberal democratic concepts.[2] Whatever their personal intentions may be, the political authorities on Taiwan must contend with expectations nourished by a constant intellectual fare of democratic ideas.

These democratic expectations have been reinforced by the influence of the United States. After 1950, when U.S. policymakers became committed to the survival of Taiwan as an advanced "outpost" of a "free world consortium," counsel and other assistance were provided by Americans who could operate effectively only in an environment that was relatively open—one that expected and fostered a reasonable flow of information between planners and the population they were expected to serve. The Sino-American Joint Commission on Rural Reconstruction (JCRR), as a case in point, was one avenue of this early influence. At the very start of Taiwan's rural modernization, American experts were instrumental in putting together the "Rule for the Organization of Village, Township, and District Farm Tenancy Committees," which established local representative associations. These associations took part in appraising the annual yields of the main crops on farmlands; from these were determined the actual farm rents to be paid during the first phases of land reform. Such associations were charged with investigating crop failures and were expected to recommend measures for reducing or even canceling farm rents in such circumstances. They also assisted in mediating disputes over the lease of farm lands.[3]

Under the influence of the JCRR, moreover, the Farmers' Associations, used by the Japanese during the colonial period as part of their control apparatus, were rehabilitated and became training grounds for political involvement. Many persons who were active in these associations went on to become elected officials—members of the provincial assembly, county magistrates, city mayors—in the subsequently established provincial and local governments.[4]

The modernization of agriculture was critical to the survival and the economic development of Taiwan, and to accomplish this modernization, American expertise and capital were essential. Moreover, since the Republic of China on Taiwan was expected to serve as a forward outpost of the "free world," it had to maintain at least a semblance of democracy. Therefore the Nationalist government, even if it had no other reason to do so, had to pay at least lip service to the democratic political predispositions of Americans. Even under crisis conditions, the Kuomintang elite could not simply renounce democratic intentions. They had to remain content with the emergency powers provided by crisis regulations, even if this was not the most effective way of ensuring the survival of the republic.

The original constitution of 1946 remains the *legal* foundation of the Republic of China to this day. More than that, however, the constitution embodies the *moral* and *ideological* warrant certifying continuity of the tradition of the revolutionary party and the revolutionary China founded by Sun Yat-sen. In the years since the founding of the republic in 1912, so many Chinese have labored, suffered, and died in the service of those revolutionary ideals that to forsake any of them would be to abandon a sacred trust.

Revolutionary parties, and the nations they create, sustain themselves in such a way. This history is the stuff out of which allegiance is fashioned. It becomes, in effect, "mythic," if a "myth" is understood not as fiction but as a brief, symbolic, and emotion-laden characterization of a people's deeply held ideals and aspirations. A "myth," understood in this sense, is the graphic and heartfelt expression of a long-term intention. It is often expressed in slogans, or in the pronouncements of a "charismatic" leader. In the Republic of China on Taiwan, political intention has found expression in such invocations as "Land to the Tillers," "The People's Livelihood," "Self-Rule for, and of, the People," and "Return to the Mainland."

Behind these slogans is the intellectual substance inherited from Sun Yat-sen. His nationalism, commitment to democracy, and programs for economic development provide the content for Taiwan's political vision. Sun sought a united, free, and eco-nomically developed China, and the leaders in Taipei see Taiwan as a microcosm, a "model province," of that greater China he envisioned. Whatever the private motives of that ruling elite might be, the moral and ideological basis of its right to rule rests exclu-sively on that vision. The commitments expressed in these social, economic, and political "myths" constitute promissory notes on the future, and their exchange value is determined by a going market rate—exchanges made with confidence between rulers and those they rule. As long as the constitution of the Republic of China remains the legal basis of the political system, the citizens of Taiwan have every legitimate right to expect the full value on the promissory notes so long in circulation.

### Fulfilling the Economic Myths

If one considers the history of Kuomintang rule on Taiwan without preconceptions, it is not hard to see how the social, eco-nomic, and political myths have shaped its behavior. The land reform and "Land to the Tillers" programs were influenced as much by ideological commitment as by "objective requirements" and the desire to legitimate Nationalist rule. Had the Kuomintang desired simply to enforce its control and ensure its tenure, it could have made use of the perfectly effective control structure left by the Japanese. The Japanese had ruled Taiwan without difficulty for fifty years by collaborating with the established landlord class, maintaining tight police control over the population, and denying the native Taiwanese access to higher education and significant positions in government. Upon assuming full control of the island, the Kuomintang could have done precisely the same thing had its purpose been simply to ensure its dominance.

But instead the Kuomintang dismantled much of the old control system by eliminating the economic base of the landlord class through land reform. By redistributing the principal assets of the island, the Nationalists orchestrated a bloodless social and political revolution. The landlords no longer rule in the countryside. Their place has been taken by a new class of small property-holders organized in Farmers' Associations and elected as representatives in the provincial and local assemblies.

General Chen Cheng, who planned and administered the entire land reform program, was a leader of the Society for the Study of Sun Yat-senism and was devoted to the principle of "The People's Livelihood." Chen worked to make the political and economic myths a reality.

The revolutionary land reform was the first stage in the massive program of economic modernization and industrial development.[5] The results of that program have made economic history. From a basically traditional agricultural society, Taiwan was transformed into one of the industrial marvels of Asia. By 1980 it had reached the threshold of industrial maturity. Per capita income exceeded U.S. $2,000. Almost every family on Taiwan owns a television set, nearly 90 per cent own refrigerators, and over 60 per cent own either an automobile or a motorcycle. The literacy rate is about 93 per cent, and life expectancy has increased from 44 years in 1949 to 72 years today. Major epidemic diseases have been all but eradicated, and health services, by Asian standards, are generous. Furthermore, the distribution of income and welfare has been remarkably equitable. The ratio of family income between the top 20 per cent and the bottom 20 per cent was 4.18 to 1 in 1978 (compared to a ratio of 9 to 1 in the United States, 29 to 1 in Ecuador, 20 to 1 in Brazil, and 15 to 1 in Mexico).[6]

## The Difficult Political Myths

By 1980, the political leadership of Taiwan had fulfilled much of the substance of the social and economic myths of "Land to the Tillers" and "The People's Livelihood." More difficult has been satisfaction of the fundamental political myth, "Self-Rule for, and of, the People." This difficulty resulted in large part from an equally compelling commitment to the imperative goal—"Return to the Mainland."

When the Nationalists moved to Taiwan, they realized that any return to the mainland would require the marshalling of all the community's resources, both material and psychological. Taiwan was to be maintained in what was substantially a state of war. The Kuomintang had not surrendered in its long conflict with Chinese Communism. It was committed to bringing Sun's "Three Principles of the People" (the principles of nationalism, the people's rights or democracy, and the people's livelihood) to the entire population of China.

This was more than an ideological commitment, for there was hardly any other option open. The victorious Communist regime on the mainland refused to countenance any alternative to a "return of Taiwan to the bosom of the Motherland." The mainland regime made it perfectly clear that it would not allow an "independent" Taiwan without massive bloodshed and oppression. How extensive the bloodshed and how intensive the oppression might be can be imagined, given the numbers killed on the mainland after the victory of Mao's forces. (The official Communist estimate was 1.8 million Kuomintang troops and nearly 1 million "bandit guerrilla forces.")

There was never an occasion, therefore, to create an independent Taiwan as an alternative to the commitment to a united China that underlies the Kuomintang call to return to the mainland. Peking would have resisted any effort to detach Taiwan from the mainland, and the United States, as the prime ally of the Taipei regime, would have been drawn into a massive and protracted confrontation with the Chinese Communists—something it was ill disposed to undertake.

But beyond these realities, there remained the vision of Sun Yat-sen that gave purpose to Nationalist rule. For the Kuomintang, Taiwan was to be a symbol of Chinese liberation—an alternative to the system established on the mainland. Taiwan was to become the "model province" of an alternative China, a concrete manifestation of what the China of the "Three Principles of the People" might be, a showplace of unity, prosperity, and democracy.[7] The political authorities in Taipei expect that economic failure and political instability will ultimately erode the "alien" Communist rule. At that point, the successes of the "model province" of Taiwan will commend it as a successor regime, and the Chinese nation will be reunited under Sun's "Three Principles."

To assume that responsibility will require the ready availability of government machinery capable of functioning for all of China. Consequently a nearly complete structure of national government is maintained on the island "province" of Taiwan, a structure brought over intact from the mainland in 1949. In the transfer to Taipei, the members of the National Assembly and the Legislative, Executive, Judicial, Control, and Examination Yuans, elected in 1947 and 1948, were ordered to take up their duties in the new "temporary" capital.

## Representative Provincial and Local Government

Below the level of this national structure there is a fully operating provincial government. In December 1951 the Taiwan Provincial Assembly was inaugurated, establishing the beginnings of local self-rule for the island's population. In 1959, the Organic Law of the Taiwan Provincial Assembly provided for the election of assembly members for renewable terms of four years by direct popular vote. Below the provincial level, also, all government offices were to be filled by popular mandate.

By the end of the fifties, therefore, Taiwan had an essentially two-tier system of government, a "national" government prepared to assume responsibilities for China in its entirety, and a provincial government occupied with the affairs of the people of the island.

The constitution of 1946 was not very specific about the makeup and powers of a provincial assembly. The Executive Yuan, by decree, established the "experimental" elements of provincial and local government, with the provincial government empowered to "pass regulations concerning the rights and obligations of the people; approve the provincial . . . budget; . . . review proposals of the provincial government; hear administrative reports of the government and make interpellations; submit proposals for administrative reforms; consider petitions from the people. . . ."[8] These powers are restricted by review procedures reserved to the Executive Yuan and by the central government's power to settle disputes between the Provincial Assembly and the provincial administration.

Below the provincial level, the assemblies of the counties, cities, townships, and rural districts exercise wide-ranging control over local government. Their regulatory power must be exerted in a manner compatible with the laws and regulations of the provincial and central governments, but they enjoy broad powers of control over their areas.

Representatives to the Provincial Assembly and to local assemblies are chosen in general elections that have evolved from disorganized and at least partly manipulated forms into better organized and increasingly fair contests. These provincial and local elections enjoy high levels of popular involvement, and there is every evidence that the electorate takes suffrage seriously.

The character of the provincial and local elections and of the assemblies those elections staff has been described as "fledgling democracy" — a serious effort to introduce democratic practices in a situation that almost everywhere else in the developing world has produced simple dictatorial rule. The Kuomintang clearly dominates both provincial and local elections; since the early sixties it has won at least 80 per cent of the seats in the Provincial Assembly, about 75 per cent of those in county and municipal assemblies, 80 per cent of the positions of magistrate and mayor in municipalities, and over 90 per cent of the headships of towns and villages.[9]

Yet the Kuomintang members elected to those positions represent a variety of factions and interest groups. The emergency regulations governing the political life on Taiwan preclude the establishment of formal opposition parties (for reasons we shall consider later). Consequently, most of those seeking election run on the established Kuomintang ticket (though there are also "non-party" candidates); advantages include access to the party's information and propaganda media and support through the party's financial resources. This means that members of various factions and interest groups pursue their special concerns under the rubric of Kuomintang membership.[10]

Examples of factional and interest-group competition dot the history of provincial and local government on the island. At times the conflict is as intense as any in multi-party systems in the West. Groups like the Farmers' Associations attempt to influence legislation in their own interest to such a degree that some lobbying scandals have occupied national attention.[11]

The restrictions on the activities of the provincial and local representatives are those that operate throughout the political system. Elected representatives are not allowed to violate any of the constraints on "subversive activities." There can be no agitation for "Taiwanese independence," no indirect or direct support for Communism, and no direct attack on the legitimacy of the central government. But even with these constraints, political life on Taiwan is dynamic. Almost all the elected officials in the provincial and local assemblies are natives of Taiwan and reflect local Taiwanese interests. Often the Provincial Assembly will generate considerable confusion, concern, and readjustment in the central government by introducing changes in the budget and entering formal questions about government regulations. In effect, while the KMT maintains a principle of party "discipline," and is generally in a position to mediate differences between interest and factional groups, there remains a reasonably wide range for the negotiation and compromise that characterize pluralistic systems.

### Permissible Forms of Opposition

The political system on Taiwan therefore entails extensive *political competition,* some *political opposition,* but little of what could be considered *opposition in principle.* The more forthright political opposition advocating extensive reform generally competes under the "non-party" label. The continuing existence of this avenue for reformist opposition is a mark of the relative openness of the system.

That there are no candidates who oppose the central government *in principle* is the result of the singular conditions governing the very existence of the Republic of China. Any persons *ideologically* opposed to Kuomintang rule would have to attempt to articulate a program that (1) sought formal independence for Taiwan, (2) promoted the Communist alternative, or (3) advocated revolutionary overthrow of the duly constituted system. All these alternatives have been categorized as "subversive," since they would invite mainland Communist intervention in Taiwanese affairs, and are therefore subject to punitive constraints.

To advocate increased democracy for the island does not, in and of itself, constitute "subversive" opposition. Such advocacy is a regular part of political criticism on Taiwan and finds expression both within and outside the Kuomintang. Other than that, the Kuomintang has been ill disposed to allow the organization of a formal opposition whose theme is increased democracy if that opposition shows any sign of being organized along the "mainlander-Taiwanese" axis. That is, the Kuomintang has been extremely sensitive to any initiative that might result in the establishment of an "ethnic" opposition—an exclusively Taiwanese political party that would exclude those Chinese and their children who left the mainland with the Nationalist government after the Communist victory.

The central government on Taiwan has worked assiduously to reduce the differences between the native Taiwanese majority and a more urban, politically aware, and politically privileged mainlander minority. One measure of its success is that native Taiwanese now make up about 75 per cent of the membership of the Kuomintang. Provincial and local governments are staffed almost entirely with native Taiwanese, as are more and more of the central government posts. Most of the development programs of the central government have enhanced the welfare and social interests of the Taiwanese, and almost all the private major economic assets of the island are in native Taiwanese hands.

Nonetheless, a residue remains of the differences that originally created population management problems for the central government. An opposition group that mobilized exclusively Taiwanese, as opposed to mainlander, allegiance, even if it did not appeal to prohibited ideological tenets, might very well create unmanageable tension.

The Kuomintang has sought to allow "principled" political competition and opposition without providing the occasion for an exclusively "native Taiwanese" opposition. Experience suggests that the latter kind of opposition often takes the form of unrealistic denunciation and obstruction bordering on simple subversion,[12] a development that would jeopardize the survival of the republic given the crisis conditions it faces. "Principled" opposition, on the other hand, fulfills useful political functions. It channels dissent peacefully, gives the central government alternative sources of information by revealing particular interests on particular policy concerns, and allows periodic tests of the central government's popularity.[13]

## The Central Government and Representation

In effect, progress toward representative democracy has continued at the provincial and local levels on Taiwan since the mid-fifties. The main problems have been at the national level. The central government is still designed to serve China in its entirety; it is understood to represent all of the nation's "occupied" provinces. Most of the representatives of those provinces were elected in 1947. They have continued to exercise legislative and control functions without having to face an electorate and have obviously become increasingly non-representative.

Furthermore, with the passage of time, their numbers have shrunk through defection, emigration, infirmity, and death. As early as 1966, the original 2,961 members of the National Assembly had dwindled to 1,488. Of the original 759 members elected to the Legislative Yuan, only about half continued to function, and those that remained were already in their sixties. While the government had to retain the character of representing all of China if the goal of the "return" was to be upheld, some change had to be made so that the democratic principles of Sun Yat-sen would not be abandoned.[14] But to disband the "long parliament" and reconstitute it with representatives elected by popular vote not only would be an implicit abandonment of the claim to represent the entire Chinese population, but also would do little more than duplicate the machinery and personnel already operating as the provincial government of Taiwan.

In the late sixties a solution was sought through "emergency supplementary elections" as well as the filling of vacancies through executive appointment. The first such election, in 1969, added fifteen new members to the National Assembly, eleven to the Legislative Yuan, and two to the Control Yuan. Given the large membership in these national bodies, these small additions through election had only a marginal impact. They were supplemented by executive appointment to fill empty seats in the National Assembly and the Legislative Yuan.[15] Yet these innovations, though very limited, were a start toward improving the representativeness of the central government.

In the early 1970s there was increased agitation for more effective representation at the national level. By that time the average age of the members of the Executive Yuan, which is essentially the cabinet of the national government, was about sixty-three, with a range from fifty-one to over seventy. The political elite of Taiwan, therefore, not only was becoming increasingly aged and infirm but represented neither the population of Taiwan nor, after more than twenty years, a constituency on the mainland of China.

When Chiang Ching-kuo became premier in 1972, he named six native Taiwanese to cabinet-level posts. Native Taiwanese were aggressively recruited for membership in the Kuomintang at a ratio equal to their ratio in the population.[16] In the same year further supplementary elections for the National Assembly and the Legislative Yuan were held.

In 1978, preparations were made once again for national elections. The members of the National Assembly and the Legislative Yuan were not required to stand for re-election, but more representatives were to be chosen from the local population.

But in mid-December, immediately before the elections were to be held, the Carter administration announced U.S. withdrawal of recognition of the Republic of China. This threw the political system into a crisis, and the elections were postponed.[17]

The diplomatic setback generated widespread internal criticism. The central government responded by closing the stock market briefly and by imposing some administrative regulations to aid adjustment to the changed situation. The most explicit form of internal dissent appeared in *Formosa Magazine (Mei-li-tao)*, where the criticism ranged over the unrepresentativeness of the political system, the persistence of one-party dominance, and the "unrealistic" and costly policy of "Return to the Mainland."[18] There was fear that the central government, still largely dominated by "mainlanders," might negotiate with the mainland Communists rather than allow the native Taiwanese to assume control over the system.[19]

## The Kaohsiung Riot

On December 10, 1979, Human Rights Day, the *Formosa Magazine* group organized a demonstration in Kaohsiung, Taiwan's second-largest city. Moved by a variety of expectations, the organizers of the demonstration chose to violate the government's strictures against a march through the city center. When the police and security forces attempted to block the proposed march, violence erupted in which 183 policemen suffered injuries. The police had been instructed not to react with force, and few of the demonstrators were hurt.

The organizers of the prohibited demonstration were charged with provoking violence and inciting to sedition. The trial was conducted in public, with local and foreign newsmen present. Representatives of some international religious and human rights groups were permitted to attend. During the trial the defendants insisted on their innocence and made the case for political reforms to satisfy the democratic aspirations of the people. They regularly alluded to the democratic spirit of Sun Yat-sen's "Three Principles of the People."

The convictions of the defendants, with sentences ranging from twelve years to life imprisonment, made clear the central government's intention not to allow dissidence to mature into an "opposition in principle." Although the dissidents had enjoyed considerable public support during their reformist opposition to the central government throughout 1979, the lapse into public violence cost them much popular favor. By the time of the Kaohsiung riot, the dissidents were seen no longer as simply reformists but as a potential source of serious political instability that might promote a cycle of reciprocal violence that could threaten the survival of the system.[20]

## The "Election and Recall Law"

The national supplementary elections that had been postponed when the United States withdrew recognition were rescheduled for December 1980. In June, the government announced its intention "not only to carry out the election but also to lay a firm foundation for democracy."[21]

The elections were to be conducted under the decree law entitled "The Public Officials Election and Recall Law," promulgated in May 1980.[22] These decree regulations resulted from consultation with more than two hundred scholars, including experts on constitutional law and specialists in comparative democratic political processes. Many American specialists were involved both formally and informally. The public press provided the opportunity for broad-based popular involvement.

The 113 articles of the "Election and Recall Law" laid out in considerable detail the conditions that were to govern the national elections. The rights and responsibilities of candidates were specified; this part of the law provided the formal legal foundation for dissident "non-party" participation. Elections of public officials were to be conducted by direct and secret ballot (art. 3), with election commissions composed of inspectors-at-large to protect against violation of voting rights (arts. 6, 7, 11, 12). Declared ineligible for public office were persons convicted of offenses "against national internal security or against national external security" or convicted of "corruption"; persons who had been proclaimed bankrupt and had not been "rehabilitated"; persons who had been "deprived of civil rights [that had] not been retrieved"; and persons who had been "proclaimed incompetent and the proclamation having not been abrogated" (art. 35).

Campaign activities for candidates for the National Assembly and the Legislative Yuan were restricted to fifteen days (art. 45). Candidates were forbidden to employ campaign assistants who were registered candidates themselves, or served as public functionaries, or had any of the disqualifications for public office specified above. No person was allowed to serve as a campaign assistant for more than one candidate (art. 47). The campaign rallies were divided into those sponsored by the candidates themselves and those organized by the election commission. No more than six campaign meetings were allowed per day, and a meeting could last no longer than two hours. The candidate himself was to conduct the meetings, and the time and place of each meeting were to be reported to the election commission three days in advance (art. 49). During campaign meetings candidates were proscribed from "instigating persons to commit offenses against the internal security or external security of the state; inciting persons to undermine social order with violence; [or] committing other offenses set forth in the criminal code" (art. 54). The procedures for casting and counting ballots were carefully stipulated to insure honesty (arts. 57-64). The rest of the law dealt primarily with the recall of elected officials.

The regulations effectively excluded any specifically ideological opposition—what we have characterized as "opposition in principle." Moreover, independent "non-party" candidates could not organize in a specifically anti-government platform that would be tantamount to an opposition party—a party that might provide the vehicle for an explicitly "ethnic" opposition vote. But other than that, the provisions were generally recognized as more progressive than any previous ones. Although candidates complained that the time allotted for campaigning was too brief, and that the constraints placed on campaign assistants were too stringent, most apparently welcomed the standardization of election procedures.

### The 1980 Campaign and Election

On November 21, 1980, 403 candidates began their campaign (five others who had registered as candidates had been disqualified on one ground or another).[23] Private campaign meetings continued until November 28, rallies organized by the election commission until December 5. The 403 candidates competed for 173 seats— 97 (23.3 per cent of the total) in the Legislative Yuan and 76 (6.2 per cent) in the National Assembly. Of the candidates for the Legislative Yuan, 55 per cent were to have been chosen by the general electorate, 17 per cent by women's groups and farmers' and workers' organizations, and 28 per cent by the overseas Chinese communities. Of the candidates for seats in the National Assembly, 70 per cent were to have been chosen by the population at large and 30 per cent by women's, farmers', and workers' associations.[24]

In addition to the Kuomintang, which fielded 254 of the 403 candidates, the Young China party and the Democratic Socialist party—recognized "opposition" parties that dated from the years on the mainland—offered candidates. "Non-party" candidates also competed, and they exceeded in both numbers and reformist zeal the candidates of the two recognized non-Kuomintang parties. The non-party candidates advocated significant changes in the political system and in domestic and foreign policies. Among them were some relatives of those convicted earlier that year in the "sedition" trials of the *Formosa Magazine* group.

The campaign headquarters of the "non-party" candidates displayed campaign propaganda that was clearly inflammatory. Cartoon posters identified the Kuomintang functionaries as corrupt and oppressive. There were allusions to the violation of civil and political rights, some of which compared the central government to the Communist regime on the mainland. At public rallies these criticisms were regularly broadcast without interference.

In general, however, most of the criticism that surfaced during the campaign turned on bread-and-butter issues. Concern was expressed over the dearth of available housing, the lack of effective labor regulation, the need for pollution control, and other matters of general welfare.

Throughout the campaign the government was singularly tolerant of criticism. The authorities had apparently made sure that neither the security services nor private organizations favoring the government interfered with the campaigning.[25]

Over 65 per cent of the eligible voters went to the polls on December 6.[26] There were no serious complaints of irregularity. The voting procedures were governed by open processes that insured conformity to established regulations. Ballots were counted in full public view. The results were publicly tallied and transmitted to election headquarters, and were conveyed to the public by the national television system.

Overall, the Kuomintang won about 80 per cent of the seats, 63 of the available 76 in the National Assembly and 56 of 97 in the Legislative Yuan. Several "non-party" candidates polled large pluralities, and some of those who had been the most controversial and the most vociferous in anti-government criticism won seats. Chou Ching-yu, the wife of one of the jailed opposition leaders, won a landslide victory for a National Assembly seat. But there was no clear and decisive opposition vote, and the Kuomintang did as well as had been expected.

The government intended that the elections "be carried out in harmony and unity"[27] and signify Taiwan's progress toward increasing democratic government. In that sense they were largely successful. The campaigning was for the most part cool, rational, and orderly. There was little rhetoric from either the extremist opposition or the government conservatives. The "non-party" candidates restricted themselves largely to "strong and constructive criticism."

The election brought new blood into the established system. Almost all the candidates, Kuomintang and non-Kuomintang alike, were native Taiwanese, and so the number of Taiwanese in the legislative bodies—the National Assembly and the Legislative Yuan—was greatly increased. In the Legislative Yuan native Taiwanese now make up about 30 per cent of the total membership and about half of the effective membership—those who regularly attend and participate in legislative sessions.

### The Future of Representative Government

The commitment to regular national elections lays the foundation for an increasingly representative national government. While the 1980 election was conducted with considerable caution and evident political restraint, it showed that the Kuomintang was prepared to allow the articulation of non-party opposition.

The previous reluctance of the Kuomintang to hold national elections did not arise from a singleminded desire to maintain control over the political system. The Kuomintang had provided for provincial and local elections since at least the early sixties and had always managed to maintain party control. What the Kuomintang has taken great pains to defend since its transfer to Taiwan is its legitimacy as the government of an alternative China. Election of an all-Taiwanese national government would hopelessly impair that legitimacy. Consequently, it is unlikely that the central government on Taiwan will *ever* accede to simple representative elections. Some provision will have to be made for at least symbolic representation of those constituencies that remain "captive" under Communist dominance on the mainland.

What we shall probably see on Taiwan in the future is the continuation of regularly scheduled national elections to fill seats vacant through age, infirmity, and death, with "reserved seats" for "symbolic" representatives of the provinces that remain under the rule of Peking. Those symbolic representatives will probably continue to be appointed by the Executive Yuan or selected by the National Assembly. Beneath that central government, the provincial assemblies (there are now three, since the cities of Taipei and Kaohsiung have achieved provincial status) and the local assemblies will be popularly elected.

The democratic process on Taiwan is clearly irreversible. Should the circumstances remain relatively stable, there will be increased liberalization of emergency controls as well.

### Increasing Native Taiwanese Participation

Chiang Ching-Kuo, who became president of the republic in 1978, has made clear his intention not only to extend democratic rights but increasingly to involve the native Taiwanese in government. As we have seen, upon becoming premier in 1972 he named six native Taiwanese to cabinet-level positions in the Executive Yuan. Three of the four vice-presidents selected in the other four branches of the central government—Legislative, Judicial,

Examination, and Control—have been native Taiwanese. A native Taiwanese, Hsieh Tung-min, was appointed governor of the province of Taiwan; his successor, Li Teng-hui, appointed in 1981, is also a Taiwanese. In the supplementary elections for the national representative bodies held in 1966, 1972, and 1980, the vast majority of successful candidates were native Taiwanese. Moreover, since the Tenth Party Congress in 1969, steps have been taken to increase native Taiwanese participation in the hierarchy of the Kuomintang. As early as 1972, three key positions were reserved for native Taiwanese. While most key positions seem to remain available to mainlanders only, nine of the twenty-seven seats in the standing central committee of the Kuomintang are now held by native Taiwanese.

None of this suggests that the Kuomintang does not maintain massive dominance in the political system, but it does suggest that change occurs. As the party and the central government include more and more native Taiwanese, the nature of government itself will inevitably change, though the change has to be gradual so as not to jeopardize the fragile security of the republic.

The Kuomintang today is no longer staffed by the survivors of China's civil war. Chiang Ching-kuo has gradually excluded the aged leaders of the past and assembled around himself a group of aggressive technocrats and leaders of Taiwan's burgeoning economy. Their perception of Taiwan's political future is significantly different from the perception of those whose memories dwell upon the protracted conflict with the Communists. Many of the young men and women around Chiang Ching-kuo are U.S.-trained university specialists long familiar with American social science and political concepts. They know about population management techniques in which political rule is seen as a function of negotiated consensus rather than heavy-handed security techniques. They fully appreciate the positive functions of controlled dissent and open lines of popular communication.

## Increasing Latitude to Critics

These young university specialists have been largely responsible for the increasing latitude afforded to public criticism of the government. In the recent past, books like Hsü Fu-kuan's 1979 *The Political Thought of the Confucian School and Democracy, Freedom and Human Rights*[28] would hardly have surfaced, much less been allowed currency. K'ang Ning-hsiang's *Six Years of Concern With Government* (1978)[29] is still available although it includes studied criticisms of the government. Hsieh Cheng-i's *Inside and Outside the Kuomintang,*[30] published in 1979-80 and highly critical of the government, remains in circulation in a new edition. The dissident publication *Liberty Bell (Tzu-yu chung)* is readily available in bookstalls. The publishing house that produces it, Pa-shih nien-tai ch'u-pan-she, issues a variety of publications including selected articles from *Free China,* a leading opposition publication of the fifties. (However, the February 1983 issue of *Pa-shih nien-tai* was banned, in part because of a memorial article on Lei Chen, publisher of *Free China*.)

Along with such non-Kuomintang criticism there is an abundance of Kuomintang criticism. Such volumes as those by T'ao Pai-ch'uan—*Taiwan Should Be Still Better* (now going into its sixth printing), *Cannot Taiwan Become Still Better?*, and *How Can Taiwan Become Still Better?* —represent criticism from the "loyal opposition."[31]

The banning of publications for violations of the emergency regulations is still fairly widespread, but sometimes the ban is applied only to particular issues of a periodical. Some banned publications still circulate freely, despite the proscription. Copies of *Formosa Magazine,* for example, are still available, though the publication is now banned.

Beyond that, a great deal of American literature is available to the English reading public of Taiwan, including books that contain either criticisms of the Kuomintang or positive assessments of the Maoist regime on the mainland. Thomas Metzger's *Escape from Predicament: Neo-Confucianism and China's Evolving Political Culture,*[32] for example, republished in Taiwan, contains a section dealing with "Mao's Achievement and the Ethos of Interdependence."

## CHAPTER SIX

# The Outlook for Human Rights in the Republic of China

*The past quarter century has brought significant advances in the observance of internationally recognized human rights on Taiwan.*

U.S. DEPARTMENT OF STATE, 1980[1]

SERIOUS RESTRICTIONS ON CIVIL and political rights remain in the Republic of China on Taiwan, but considerable progress has been made. Full restitution of civil and political rights will probably not occur so long as the island remains under the threat of military attack and subversion by Peking. Yet there are areas in which further progress can be made.

One such area is the entire judicial system, its independence, and its capacity to protect the civil and political rights of the citizens even under the weight of emergency regulations. The courts on Taiwan have only a short history of operating by Western concepts of law. Traditional Chinese governance placed great emphasis on a system of ethics rather than a code of law.[2] The first modern legal code drafted in China, a code of company law, did not appear until 1904. Thereafter, through revolution and war, codes of civil, maritime, bankruptcy, and criminal law were drafted, and by the end of World War II the legal codes of the Republic of China compared favorably with those of any Western nation.[3] With the transfer to Taiwan, development of the legal codes continued, largely under the influence of the American legal system.[4]

## Judicial Protection of Rights

The basis for the rule of law, then, has been reasonably well established on Taiwan. What seems to be most lacking is an aggressive judicial defense of individual rights. While the Council of Grand Justices of the Republic of China (the functional equivalent of the U.S. Supreme Court) has the power of judicial review and is thus empowered to protect the civil and political rights of individuals under the 1946 constitution, the grand justices have not shown great enterprise in discharging that responsibility. Between 1950 and 1975 the Council of Grand Justices received 110 applications submitted by individuals for judicial review, but only one resulted in a constitutional ruling. The other applications were rejected either as frivolous or for not meeting procedural or jurisdictional requirements.[5]

In 1976, however, the Council of Grand Justices began to show more of a disposition to deal with petitions submitted by individual citizens. Four applications were accepted and acted upon; though the decisions rendered were unfavorable to the petitioners, the fact that the applications were adjudicated on their merits may signal a significant change in the council's attitude. At least two of these petitions turned on the constitutionality of judicial precedents rather than simple matters of administrative ordinance, and were consequently of general significance. Should the council be prepared to undertake such judicial obligations, citizens might expect increased protection for civil and political constitutional rights in the future.

To date, most of the council's work has dealt with clarifying terminology used in the constitution in response to applications made by government agencies. The grand justices have devoted much less time and energy to the major matter of judging the constitutionality of statutes or ordinances; only six of the fifty-six cases submitted by government agencies and adjudicated by the council in the past thirty years involved constitutionality.

## "Ex Post Facto" Prosecution

Some of the council's decisions have had major constitutional significance. For example, three of its constitutional interpretations dealt with the proscription against *ex post facto* prosecution in criminal proceedings.

The criminal code of the Republic of China states that acts are punishable "only if expressly so provided by the law in force at the time of . . . commission." This excludes *ex post facto* prosecution. Moreover, article 2 of the code provides that if the law in force at the time of trial is different from that in force at the time of commission of the crime, the law more favorable to the defendant shall apply.

The emergency regulations allow for the apprehension and prosecution of any person who has, at any time, been a member of a "rebellious organization" or "attended a meeting of such organization." Many citizens of the Republic of China might therefore find themselves subject to prosecution for acts undertaken decades before—in some cases before such acts had been forbidden. Moreover, under the emergency regulations, such cases would be prosecuted in military courts, where the proceedings would be more summary and the punishment more severe.

In this area, then, the emergency regulations effectively nullify a central guarantee of the criminal code. The Council of Grand Justices was asked to decide whether this nullification was constitutional.

In its decisions, the council has allowed the application of the emergency regulations in this area, limiting the safeguards against retroactivity provided in the criminal code to instances involving ordinary criminals. In other words, citizens are protected against *ex post facto* prosecution only for common criminal offenses. If they are charged with violating the emergency regulations they can be apprehended, prosecuted in military courts, and punished—with heavier penalties than those prescribed by the civilian criminal code—for acts committed decades before, when such acts may not have been illegal.

The rationale to which the council has appealed in these decisions turns on the crisis conditions that necessitated the emergency regulations. The council has defined Taiwan's present circumstances as tantamount to a "state of siege." In such a state, the national community requires special provisions for its defense against a mortal threat. Although the civilian courts still function, they are not expeditious enough or severe enough to serve as deterrents against "subversive elements." A "state of siege" has the character of a long test of strength, in which the threatened community is required to maintain a high level of vigilance. In such circumstances, it may well be necessary to treat political offenses with special severity. In a crisis situation with the features of a siege, the survival of the community takes precedence over the protection of individual civil and political rights. Exceptional procedures and the use of military rather than civilian courts in the prosecution of "sedition" are therefore seen as warranted.[6]

The Council of Grand Justices, the supreme court of the Republic of China, has thus justified the use of retroactive culpability in cases involving political offenses against the emergency regulations. Unlike the Anglo-Saxon countries, the ROC follows the civil law procedures of continental Europe, and the courts are not empowered to determine the extent or duration of an emergency. That power resides exclusively with the executive and legislative branches of government. The Council of Grand Justices cannot, therefore, declare an emergency resolved; it can only render judgments on the emergency regulations—their proportionality and the cogency of the rationale supporting them. But the council has not even exercised its prerogatives in assessing the proportionality of the emergency measures. The kinds of offenses that can be tried by military courts have been reduced not by judicial intervention but by actions of the executive or legislative branches.

Despite the council's apparent reluctance to undertake a more aggressive general defense of individual civil and political rights, one might have expected at least a spirited opposition to the use of retroactivity in prosecutions for sedition. As the law is currently applied, it is still possible for a 65-year-old man to be charged with sedition for having briefly been a member of the Communist party of China in his youth. A citizen who has given every evidence of loyalty for thirty years can be apprehended and punished for something he did decades ago. The threat of retroactive punishment can hardly have any deterrent effect on the current spread of subversive ideas. It can only generate ill will and promote anxiety.

Retroactivity is generally considered objectionable in principle and has long been condemned in both civil and common law. In American jurisprudence, *ex post facto* laws are generally held to be void in and of themselves.

The Council of Grand Justices could, of course, cite cases in which the courts of the United States have allowed resident aliens to be deported because of prior (and sometimes many years prior) membership in the Communist party (or other "criminal organizations"). But these cases have dealt either with resident aliens or with persons who had acquired citizenship under false pretenses. Furthermore, such instances have been roundly criticized (particularly in the 1924 Supreme Court case of *Mahler* v. *Ebby*), for retroactivity is a suspect means of ensuring security. The Council of Grand Justices of the Republic of China would be well advised to find *ex post facto* measures unconstitutional under a system that aspires to the Western concept of the rule of law.

This cannot be taken to mean that a democratically constituted state does not enjoy the right of self-preservation. When the Federal Republic of Germany declared the Communist party illegal, German citizens petitioned the European Court of Human Rights for relief from what they understood to be violations of their rights according to the European Convention on Civil and Political Rights. But the European Court held such a proscription allowable under the right of democratic self-defense. Such proscriptions have no retroactive effect, however.

In principle, there can be no objection to the proscription against membership in the Communist party, or similarly disposed parties, in the ROC. The Communist party of China has never abandoned its ultimate goal of bringing Taiwan under the dominance of Peking, and the threat of Communist use of violence, terror, and military force remains very real. The Republic of China on Taiwan has every reason to see the continuing threat of infiltration, subversion, and violence as a menace to its survival and to the well-being of its citizens, and the laws must provide the restraints appropriate to the dangers. But at the same time a government under the rule of law should not unnecessarily reduce the rights characteristic of democratic systems.

## The Publication Law

The Council of Grand Justices has also been asked to pass on the constitutionality of the Publication Law, which provides for the censorship constraints. Before beginning publication, every new magazine and newspaper in Taiwan must register with a local or provincial government agency and then obtain a publishing license from the Government Information Office of the Executive Yuan. If at any time a publication carries "offending" material, the government is empowered to levy fines, confiscate copies, or take other measures against it. Such sanctions, which may include a ban on publication for up to one year, are meted out against publications conceived as inciting "a person to commit offenses against the internal security of the state, interference with public functions, voting, or public order, [or] offenses against morals or religion." Since the ROC constitution explicitly guarantees freedom of the press, the Control Yuan appealed to the Council of Grand Justices to decide on the constitutionality of the Publication Law.

The council judged that the Publication Law was inoffensive on the basis of article 23 of the constitution, which provides that "all the freedoms and rights enumerated in the preceding articles shall not be restricted by law except by such as may be necessary to prevent infringement upon the freedom of other persons; to avert an imminent crisis; to maintain social order; or to advance the public welfare."

In effect, the council argued for the constitutionality of the Publication Law on the same grounds allowed for limits on civil and political rights in the International Covenant on Civil and Political Rights, the Universal Declaration of Human Rights, and the European Convention for the Protection of Human Rights and Fundamental Freedoms. As we have seen, article 4 of the International Covenant allows restrictions on rights "in time of public emergency which threatens the life of the nation. . . ." In article 29 of the Universal Declaration of Human Rights, a variant of this qualifier is expressed as follows:

> In the exercise of his rights and freedoms, everyone shall be subject only to such limitations as are determined by law solely for the purpose of securing due recognition and respect for the rights and freedoms of others and meeting the just requirements of morality, public order, and the general welfare. . . .

And in article 10 of the European Convention, this is similarly expressed:

> The exercise of these freedoms [in which the freedom of expression is included] . . . may be subject to such formalities, conditions, restrictions, or penalties as are prescribed by law and are necessary in a democratic society, in the interests of national security, territorial integrity, or public safety, for the prevention of disorder or crime, for the protection of health or morals, for the protection of the reputation or rights of others, for preventing the disclosure of information received in confidence, or for maintaining the authority and impartiality of the judiciary.

### The Administrative Court

Since the Council of Grand Justices upheld the constitutionality of the Publication Law, the range of freedom of expression allowed is determined by administrative judgment. Any relief from infringements must therefore be sought not in the Council of Grand Justices but in the Administrative Court, which has the exclusive power to adjudicate administrative matters. The system is similar to the administrative court systems of Italy, the Federal Republic of Germany, and Austria. In such systems the administrative courts are distinct from the courts of civil justice. They deal with disputes between government agencies, and between these agencies and the general population.

Persons seeking redress from administrative actions restricting their freedom of expression can appeal to the Administrative Court. The record of the court to date, however, shows scant protection for individual rights. Since 1959 the rate of dismissal for petitions of redress in general has never fallen below 80 per cent.[7] This is unfortunate, since the Administrative Court would seem to provide a law-governed arena in which citizen complaints could be reviewed in a dispassionate and equitable manner. The Administrative Court might hear, for example, the complaints of authors like Yao Chia-wên, whose criticisms of the regulations governing "sedition" appeared in the inaugural issue of the subsequently banned *Formosa Magazine*.[8] In the adversary proceeding in the court, the legal representatives of the government could fully articulate the justification for the restrictions embodied in the "anti-sedition" emergency regulations. The case would have to be as detailed and as explicit as possible, crafted to convince the disinterested observer.

The least that citizens can expect of their government is a studied public vindication of any limitations on civil and political rights. The substantive treatment of citizen complaints about restrictions on freedom of expression would provide the occasion for such a vindication. The arguments advanced by intellectuals such as Yao Chia-wên merit a thorough government response, and the Administrative Court would seem to offer the appropriate environment for such a response.

Similarly, the arguments rendered by the dissident press concerning national economic policies[9] should be considered by the Administrative Court if those arguments constitute the grounds for administratively imposed sanctions. If the sanctions imposed are the consequence of the writers' insistence upon the availability of Marxist literature,[10] or their incitement to "class hatred,"[11] those grounds should be clearly and publicly stated. Criticism of government policy in and of itself can hardly qualify as a security offense unless it can be shown that such criticism is irresponsible and specifically designed to provoke public unrest.

It is evident that the government would have every advantage in making such arguments before the Administrative Court. Given the threats with which the Republic of China on Taiwan must contend, it seems equally evident that the government's arguments would prevail. But such an exchange would tend to reduce arbitrariness in applying the restrictions found in the Publication Law.

In providing more opportunities for citizens to challenge the behavior of government agencies, the Administrative Court would provide the people with greater protection against unnecessary restrictions of their democratic rights. The court could act as a relatively sensitive but responsible arbiter in determining what might be considered "seditious" and "subversive" public expression, and in providing reasonable assessments of the threat represented by one or another publication or public speech. Matters like these should not be left exclusively to simple administrative discretion. Such institutionalized procedures would surely be sensitive enough to block potentially dangerous materials, and yet they would allow citizens to gain confidence in a system of law that offered them some assurance of protection.

Constructive criticism of the entire judicial system on Taiwan has become commonplace, and as a result jurisdiction over the courts has been transferred from the Executive to the Judicial Yuan—a move calculated to increase their independence. More recently, amendments to the Code of Criminal Procedures provide suspects with the right to the advice and counsel of an attorney during the preliminary investigation that precedes formal indictment. In effect, considerable progress has been made, and there is good reason to believe that progress will continue in the direction of increased protection for the civil and political rights of the citizens of the ROC.

### The Possibility of Free Labor Unions

Limitations of space do not permit discussion of all the matters that merit assessment. The right of free association, however, a fundamental right in a democratic society, requires some comment. As much as restrictions on this right may be justified by the protracted crisis conditions on Taiwan, some new developments can be expected in the near future. There is little likelihood that a formally constituted opposition party will be allowed to organize. But the reorganization and revitalization of free labor unions is a likely possibility for several reasons.

In the period of liberalization that followed the accession of Chiang Ching-kuo to the premiership in 1972, the Chinese Federation of Labor was reconstituted. A new labor law was promulgated that not only allows the voluntary organization of labor unions but, in principle, allows them to strike in the pursuit of their interests. In practice, however, the labor unions organized to date give every appearance of being "company unions," labor associations fostered and maintained by business. Such company-organized and -controlled associations have been traditionally recognized as compliant tools of management. Their executives and shop stewards are housed on establishment premises and enjoy privileges in work and salary; consequently they tend to be solicitious of company, rather than worker, interests. Moreover, under the existing law, the strike option can be exercised by any labor union only with the unanimous consent of its members, and only when the wage scale offered by management falls below the very low levels established by the government. As currently constituted, and under prevailing legislation, such labor organizations cannot be realistically expected to serve as aggressive champions of the interests of their members.[12]

So far this has not been a particular disability, because wage levels have increased more rapidly than levels of productivity, given the shortage of labor, the low level of unemployment, and Taiwan's economic expansion. But in view of probable future economic conditions, and the scandalously low wages paid to women, this will probably change. How the political authorities face this matter will be an important factor in the development of a substantially democratic political system.

These, then, are some of the areas of potential change in the ROC. All things considered, the political system has made considerable progress toward increased democratic freedoms since its inception in 1949. That progress has been aided and fostered by American influence. Official U.S. participation in the construction of the system through the influence of American experts on joint commissions, American advice and counsel through the various foreign service agencies on Taiwan, American training of an entire class of educated Chinese, and the indirect impact of American literature and opinion have all contributed to the process. The legal system on Taiwan bears innumerable traces of American concepts of jurisprudence, the economic system is heavy with American practices, and the political system is alive with the phraseology of American ideals. This influence and the legacy of Sun Yat-sen create an environment conducive to the growth of political democracy.

The citizens of the Republic of China on Taiwan enjoy far more of the social and economic rights advanced in the Universal Declaration of Human Rights and in the International Covenant on Economic, Social, and Cultural Rights than citizens of any Marxist regime and more than those in some authoritarian regimes in Asia and Africa. But more important, they enjoy those human rights along with more abundant civil and political freedoms.

CHAPTER SEVEN

# *Human Rights and U.S. Foreign Policy*

*[In] Communist countries . . . ideology places the matter of
human rights in a perspective altogether different from our
own. The Communists are the practiced users of a
double-speak that can take what we deem to be violations of
personal liberty as steps toward a more ideal social system.
Their violations of human rights are always redeemed in the
ultimate vistas of history, the secret truth of which they are in
sole possession. No case of ordinary human rights could be
presented strong enough to dent the self-righteous armor of
their apocalyptic vision of the socialist future.*

WILLIAM BARRETT[1]

SEVERAL TENTATIVE CONCLUSIONS EMERGE from the historical analysis in this study. One is that whatever role the human
rights issue plays in the future, American foreign policy-makers
cannot pretend that "internationally recognized human rights" can
provide an unambiguous guide to conduct.[2] Not only are the
United Nations deliberative bodies responsible for these international codes hopelessly politicized, but many of the notions of
"internationally recognized human rights" that prevail in ideocratic regimes either are inimical to the fundamental civil and political
rights enjoyed in pluralist communities, or afford the occasion for
violating an entire catalogue of individual and collective rights
accepted in common international practice.

The Soviet Union and Communist China have effectively used
the human rights issue to support political arrangements that sys-

tematically, and in principle, deny individual human rights in support of "collective rights." By claiming to seek to provide "more advanced" social and economic rights, they have obscured the fact that the denial of individual civil and political rights is intrinsic to revolutionary Marxist regimes. The U.N. General Assembly has accepted much of the substance of Soviet and Communist Chinese arguments and has thereby acquiesced in the degrading of civil and political rights while providing little support for the social and economic rights that this degradation was supposed to purchase.

The concept of "internationally recognized human rights" is simply too unwieldy and too ambiguous to be used in any effective policy. The U.S. foreign policy-making establishment will have to formulate a comprehensive program of its own if it wishes to further the development of civil and political rights in allied, neutral, and adversary states.

Yet the fact remains that the withholding of economic or security support for recognized violators of "internationally recognized human rights" is built into current U.S. legislation. Each year the Department of State must provide Congress with "country reports" detailing the observance or nonobservance of internationally recognized human rights in all countries that receive U.S. economic or security assistance and in all other members of the United Nations. The reports evaluate the human rights performance of each country in two categories: (1) respect for the integrity of the person, including freedom from killing, from torture, from cruel, inhuman, or degrading treatment or punishment, from arbitrary arrest or imprisonment, from denial of fair public trial, and from invasion of the home; (2) respect for civil and political liberties, including freedom of speech, press, assembly, and religion; freedom of movement within the country, foreign travel, emigration, and repatriation; and freedom to participate in the political process. A third section describes the government's attitude toward outside investigations of its human rights practices, while a fourth comments on economic and social conditions such as life expectancy, literacy rate, per capita GNP, and the percentage of the population living in poverty. (The 1982 reports on the People's Republic of China and the Republic of China on Taiwan appear in the appendix of this book; see page 107.)

Most of the reporting requirements mandated by U.S. legislation have to do with "traditional" or "classic" rights, the basic civil and political rights, protected in the International Covenant on Civil and Political Rights even under circumstances that allow the suspension of other, less fundamental rights in times of emergency.[3] These are rights that have traditionally been recognized in U.S. laws and practices.

In the European Convention for the Protection of Human Rights and Fundamental Freedoms, the same catalogue of rights appears, in three classes: (1) No derogation is allowed from basic rights to the security of life, protection against torture and cruel or degrading treatment, and guarantees against retroactive culpability, even under emergency conditions. (2) Standard civil and political rights of expression, association, impartial and public trial, and the inviolability of the home are privileged, and derogation is allowed only under emergency conditions. Finally (3), there are vital needs to be filled as resources and circumstances allow.

## HUMAN RIGHTS IN IDEOCRATIC SYSTEMS

The twentieth century has seen the gross violation of the first class of rights, the most fundamental ones, with an alarming frequency. The fury of mass murder that has eliminated millions from the earth in this century is perhaps without parallel in history. Many if not most of these instances of mass destruction of innocents have occurred in ideocratic systems, systems that deny the very existence of inherent rights.

Both purposeful and indiscriminate murder of thousands, even millions, can occur in the frenzy of revolution. In the Soviet Union as many as 14 million persons may have died in the civil war and in the famine that followed.[4] On the mainland of China, perhaps as many as a million "bad gentry" died in the "land reforms" prior to 1949, and the Communist Chinese themselves estimate that as many as 5 million persons were "eradicated" immediately after the military victory over the Nationalists. In the Pakistan civil war, as many as a million Bengalis were butchered. Hundreds of thousands, perhaps millions, of innocents died in the tribal and secessionist wars that have marred the recent history of Africa.

But only in ideocratic regimes have such horrors continued, sometimes with increased frenzy, after the secure establishment of the state. While mass expulsions have been common as an aftermath of war both within states and between states, in the recent past it has been only in ideocratic environments that "class enemies" have continued to suffer for years and decades after public order has been secured. Only in such regimes have whole populations been forced to flee through expulsion or political and economic harassment. Over twenty years after the victory of the "Cuban Revolution," 125,000 refugees were forced to flee Cuba. For years after the revolution that "liberated" their countries, hundreds of thousands of refugees were finding their hazardous way out of socialist Vietnam and Marxist Laos.

Hitler's massacre of the Jews was not the consequence of revolutionary violence. It was cold, calculated government policy. Stalin's murder of as many as 15 million Soviet citizens was not the consequence of revolutionary self-defense.[5] It was a calculated policy of terror to purge purported "class enemies." Mao's murder of over a million Chinese during the "Great Leap Forward" and three million more during the "Great Proletarian Cultural Revolution" occurred long after the Communist regime was secure from any serious "counterrevolutionary" attempt.[6] The millions who have perished in labor camps in the Soviet Union and in Communist China did not die in a revolutionary upheaval but were willfully sacrificed to some ideological vision.

Similarly, when Pol Pot announced in September 1977 that the "reactionary elements" in Kampuchea would be either "educated," "neutralized," or "eradicated"[7] and proceeded to murder over a million—perhaps over two million—persons subject to his control, this was not the consequence of fear of counterrevolution. Pol Pot was acting out the dictates of a policy of "ruralization" and "purification" that was both anti-urban and anti-capitalist.

The grossest violations of human rights in practice occur in systems that deny human rights in principle. During the tragic years of Stalin's "great purges," Administrative Boards, composed of members of the Ministry of Internal Affairs, could mete out sentences of up to twenty-five years without trial and with no possible appeal for "anti-Soviet agitation," "suspicion of espionage," "counterrevolutionary thought," "dissemination of anti-Soviet sentiments," or being "members of a criminal family."[8]

On the Chinese mainland, for over thirty years, punishments were imposed with no reference to criminal codes. Thirty to forty million persons suffered systematic discrimination because they derived from "black class backgrounds." How many hundreds of thousands remain in "thought reform" labor camps under the present "reformist" Communist regime is a matter of speculation.

## HUMAN RIGHTS IN AUTHORITARIAN SYSTEMS

Homicidal violence, mass expulsions, and other violations of human rights often attend the first phases of authoritarian rule; but generally such regimes rapidly settle into simple mistreatment of individuals, and some return to a constitutional order that assures at least minimal civil and political rights. Evolution into an ordered pluralistic system always remains a possibility. Authoritarian regimes tend to be non-ideological—"pragmatic" and "realistic." In general they tend to maintain the fundamentals of a market economy, which opens their systems to international scrutiny. Ideocratic regimes, in contrast, almost always impose a command economy on their populations and hermetically seal them from the prying eyes of "foreign interference."

The violence on Taiwan that took many thousands of lives during the rebellion of February 28, 1947, was a flashpoint in the very early history of the regime—before political order and stability had been established. Since then there have been occasional riots, charges of torture, and "disappearances" of political opponents, but nothing remotely akin to the mass murders and expulsions that have figured so prominently in the post-revolutionary history of Marxist regimes. The mixed economic system on Taiwan allows extensive and continuous foreign contacts, and that influence has helped to moderate the control measures used by the regime.

But more determinative than the "pragmatism" and the relative permeability of the regime is the rooting of the legitimacy of

Kuomintang rule in the normative conceptions of Sun Yat-sen. Among the last affirmations Sun left to his intellectual heirs was that "everyone is endowed by nature with human rights [jen-chüan]. . . ."[9] A little earlier he had insisted that "all humanity shares the same essence; being alike, everyone is entitled to equality and freedom."[10] And as early as 1906 he had maintained that "equality and liberty are a people's natural rights."[11]

These affirmations provide the ethical foundations of government, and establish the natural-law presumption that supports human rights. However long those rights may be suspended because of emergency conditions, their ultimate restoration is implicit in the commitment to equality and freedom.

Revolutionary Marxist systems offer no such promise. Stalinists, Marxist-Leninists, Maoists, and Cuban *fidelistas* have all rejected any notion of inherent human rights that might take precedence over substantive political and social goals. In their scheme, normative claims are all derivative of some incontestible political purpose. As a consequence, all the official "constitutions" that provide the legal bases for ideocratic systems make human rights—civil, political, social, economic, or cultural—contingent upon the forbearance of the political elite. There is no anticipation of a time when a return of "normal" conditions would require the restoration of inherent civil and political rights. Political legitimacy is based on adherence to the ideology of the "founders" (whoever they might be considered to be at any given time) of revolutionary Marxism. To date, no such system has reinterpreted the founders so as to acknowledge the legitimacy of "inalienable" human rights.[12]

In contrast, authoritarian systems—if they are not strictly traditional monarchies or sheikdoms—will generally incorporate some elements of "natural rights" into their rationale for rule. Most of them do not have an articulated ideology, and so the concept of natural rights becomes a useful alternative. Most of the military-bureaucratic authoritarian states of Latin America, for example, embrace some significant elements of the "inherent human rights" doctrines in their founding documents. This allows the possibility that they might some day accede to foreign or domestic persuasion and permit such rights. That would require only an alteration of practice—though perhaps a profound alteration. For a revolutionary Marxist regime to provide fundamental civil and political rights would require not only a substantial change in practice but also an abandonment of cardinal ideological principles.

In the recent past we have seen authoritarian systems impose and lift emergency restraints on civil and political rights. Some have even made a successful transition, however unstable, from authoritarianism to a respectable pluralism. Francoist Spain is the most notable instance, but the Republic of China on Taiwan seems to have gone a long way toward political pluralism.

Because authoritarian systems are relatively open to foreign influence, the United States has been able to foster official respect for civil and political rights in them. In providing assistance for economic modernization programs on Taiwan, for example, Americans transmitted political attitudes and skills as well. In providing legal counseling, Americans influenced the development of business and criminal codes in the direction of the rule of law. The Chinese of Taiwan were taught that an unimpeded flow of technical information provides the environment for increased economic efficiency. This concept of free exchange tends to carry over into the political sphere.

This suggests that market-system authoritarianism permits the United States both directly and indirectly to encourage the development of a political system that allows for increased public participation. A market economy fosters active interest-group involvement, which invariably has political influence. What this tends to mean in most developing authoritarian states is that the entrepreneurial and financial sectors of the population have considerable influence while peasants and workers have little. As a consequence, there is a tendency for inequalities of wealth to become greater.[13]

Among the developing economies, the Republic of China on Taiwan has had perhaps the most equitable distribution of family income. It is more equitable than the distribution in many of the more developed socialist states, and certainly more than that on the Chinese mainland. Sun's normative injunctions concerning natural rights and equality are manifest in the tendency toward income equity.[14]

An authoritarian system that conceives of certain civil, political, and economic rights as inherent and that allows Americans to exert practical influence by providing assistance in agricultural and industrial development affords the most fertile ground for the promotion of human rights. Unfortunately, these favorable conditions do not always exist. Either (1) the developing system has no commitment to human rights or income equality, or (2) economic factors make the reduction of economic inequality very difficult to pursue, or (3) foreign influence is exerted only through the provision of capital instead of through the kind of protracted exchange that has typified the Taiwan experience, or, (4) worse still, the system administers foreign assistance through bureaucratic agencies that systematically reinforce centralized control.[15]

In such authoritarian systems, the political system becomes increasingly primitive, and more and more the regulation of daily life becomes a responsibility of the security forces. Interest groups can no longer express their concerns, and frustration mounts. The resulting resistance is often suppressed by violence and leads to heavy-handed intervention by the government in all aspects of public life.

Political development must accompany economic development if a regime is to enjoy stability.[16] A political system has become stable when a substantial part of the population thinks its needs are met by the institutions that are a part of the system.[17] A system can attain this stability in several ways. One is through the elimination of all real or potential opponents, followed by the creation of a single party and an omnipresent bureaucracy that can co-opt all the surviving intellectual talent. This bureaucracy then allocates benefits, penalties, and information, thus approximating its objective of absolute security. Periodic purges and campaigns for thought reform allow the system to survive economic, political, and diplomatic disasters that would unseat any other form of political rule. Communist China is one of the most dramatic examples of this absolute rule.

Market-based authoritarian systems, by contrast, must legitimate their rule by satisfying the overt needs of at least a substantial portion of the population. To do this, they must develop institutionalized means for gathering, communicating, and acting upon relevant information. Such systems then become increasingly complex. As the process of economic development proceeds, traditional sectors of the society undergo fundamental change, and new needs arise. Groups within the population that formerly were passive become energized by such changes as urbanization. The need for detailed information increases, and so some means of assessing public sentiment must be developed. Interest groups must be allowed to form and to express their interests. In effect, there must be some measure of freedom of association and expression, protected by legal safeguards. The ROC on Taiwan reflects just this kind of evolution.

Without these adjustments, a system begins to decay.[18] It cannot collect information, assess threats, offset opposition, or allocate resources efficiently. Even the economic environment becomes unpredictable. The political system becomes more and more primitive in its response patterns, and ultimately it responds exclusively through organs of repression—the police, the military, and the secret services. The balance of response and coercion characteristic of all political systems[19] tilts dramatically toward coercion. The fragility of such systems is evident in the recent history of rapid and unexpected revolutions in Iran and Nicaragua.

## THE TAIWAN EXAMPLE

The development of Taiwan provides a dramatic contrast to this downward spiral. Like Iran in the mid-fifties, Taiwan undertook a program of land reform, agricultural modernization, and rapid economic development. For a variety of reasons (not the least of which was a complex and island-wide rehabilitation of village, township, and district farmers' associations), agricultural development on Taiwan was an almost unparalleled success.[20] The landlord class was made less influential and was partially compensated. Rising farm incomes permitted significant improvement in rural living standards. Prices remained stable. At the same time, an elaborate economic infrastructure was built (with U.S. advice and concessional aid) that allowed rural areas both to benefit from improved amenities and to participate in the first stages of industrialization.

Adequate transportation and communication and a sufficient energy supply at constant prices, built on a substantial base inherited from the Japanese, enabled industry to employ surplus or underemployed rural workers at attractive cost levels.[21] Rural inhabitants could add to family income by commuting to industrial plants, and the exodus from rural areas was controlled. Until the mid-seventies the ratio of rural to urban populations had not changed significantly from the early fifties, when economic modernization began in earnest.

At the same time the rapid growth of domestic industry enabled former landowners to invest money they had received for their land in modern enterprises and in urban real estate, both promising substantial rewards. Labor in the cities earned wages at levels that reflected increased productivity. Members of the growing intelligentsia were free to emigrate if they could not find attractive opportunities at home. In the growing system, expanding at a rate second only to that of Japan, the bureaucracy provided employment for those with management and planning skills. The military was rendered totally subordinate to civilian control.

The most important interest groups in the system were allowed to organize. Business and financial associations grew, and the provincial and district assemblies were organized. An elaborate statistical monitoring of all aspects of the society was set up to provide the data for effective planning and social policies. This flow of information enabled the government to respond deftly to early signals in the economy and elsewhere.

As local industry saturated the small domestic market, the government initiated a program of import duty rebates, and it stimulated export-led growth through a complex policy of loan and tax incentives. Government-sponsored research agencies provided management and planning skills so that the transition to an industrial economy was cost-efficient and minimally dislocating. As industry became increasingly dominant, rural income declined, and so the government initiated agricultural price support policies to maintain equitable income levels throughout the system. Through the eighties, agricultural family income is not expected to fall below 70 per cent of urban family income. Political and civil liberties have been warily but effectively extended. Much of the old machinery of political control has been modified, and at present the vast majority of the Chinese on Taiwan have little if any occasion to encounter police or security agencies.

All this has produced a remarkably stable political system even in the face of a protracted and demanding crisis involving military, subversive, and economic hazards.

When the dissidents of the *Formosa* group organized their protests in December 1979, many of the demonstrators saw a similarity between the situation on Taiwan and that in Iran immediately preceding the "Islamic Revolution." But the entire development of the ROC attests to fundamental differences between the two.

There is very little determined opposition to the political system on Taiwan. Where such opposition exists elsewhere, the most repressive authoritarian systems have seldom been able to contain it. The Shah could not contain it, nor could Somoza in Nicaragua. Unlike ideocratic systems, authoritarian regimes do not have institutionalized means for massive and effective purges. Their survival therefore depends on at least passive support. Where that support is not forthcoming, the system degenerates into revolutionary crisis. The primitive measures available to authoritarian regimes—counterinsurgency, assassinations, and heavy-handed repression—very often simply exacerbate resistance.

Those circumstances clearly did not exist in Taiwan in 1979, do not now exist, and have not existed there for a long time. The indications are that a strong reformist program is capable of attracting considerable support on Taiwan, but a truly revolutionary constituency is absent. Most of the reformists—like those who staff the principal opposition publications—are disaffected intellectuals with a very limited support base in the general community. Why this is so is fairly obvious. In its 1980 "Country Reports on Human Rights Practices," the Department of State asserts:

Taiwan has established an excellent record of fostering the economic rights of its people. Public policies have helped promote growth accompanied by a narrowing of the gap between the rich and the poor. . . . Taiwan's low unemployment rate reflects great employment opportunities for the population. In mid-1980, average monthly wages for employees [were] . . . almost double the 1976 level. Rising real wages have meant a higher standard of living. . . . To provide better protection for workers, the authorities currently are drafting a new labor law. . . .

Taiwan has been very successful in meeting the rights of its population to a standard of living that is adequate for health and well-being. . . . In the area of housing, the Taiwan authorities have included major expenditures for public housing under a 1976-1982 development plan. . . . Although some persons continue to live in substandard or slum conditions, the situation has greatly improved, and most people can now afford adequate housing. The right to education is one of the main concerns of the authorities and the population in general. . . . As in many societies, gaps exist between the conditions in the cities and the countryside, but the authorities are attempting to reduce these disparities.[22]

Because of all this, Taiwan enjoys remarkable stability for a community in protracted crisis. Barring direct intervention by the forces from mainland China, future changes in Taiwan will most likely be incremental and evolutionary rather than revolutionary.

## IMPLICATIONS FOR U.S. POLICY

The story of the Republic of China on Taiwan suggests that American political ideals can be most influential in developing countries through programs of economic assistance and low-profile legal counseling. Through effective joint programs in agricultural development or industrial planning, the principle of popular participation can be associated with successful performance. This inevitably has an effect upon the political process. The U.S. interest in furthering the cause of human rights in evolving authoritarian systems is best associated with a concern for the stability of the system. Such an interest can most effectively be promoted at the level of aid agencies and area desks, rather than through public scolding by senior officials and stentorian appeals to abstract ideals—which often sound either threatening or destabilizing and always have a tinge of arrogance.

For authoritarian regimes attempting rapid economic modernization, the argument that increased popular participation in developmental programs is a valuable information asset that can help a regime to function better is clearly more persuasive than an appeal to the moral requirement that "democratic rights" be restored. When popular participation can be shown to be effective, human rights can only benefit—and the ultimate strategic and economic interests of the United States are served as well.

Human rights concerns can and should be incorporated into every aspect of U.S. humanitarian, security, and development assistance. But that involvement must be discreet and substantive rather than punitive and hortatory. When the Congress has imposed punitive riders on American assistance, those riders have often done little more than provoke rejection by the prospective aid recipients. Several Latin American countries—including Brazil, Chile, Argentina, and Peru—have simply refused U.S. aid when punitive "imperialist stipulations" were appended.

In fact, the United States really has very little opportunity to compel developing nations to respect human rights through punitive restrictions on foreign aid. In the principal and critically important Latin American countries, for example, U.S. aid has substantially decreased. Loans and grants to Brazil declined from $329 million in 1966 to a scant $17.2 million in 1974. Brazil would be unlikely to revise any of its internal policies to secure that amount of aid. The situation is much the same with Argentina, Colombia, Mexico, Peru, and Venezuela. In Latin America, only Chile, Haiti, and El Salvador remain major recipients of U.S. foreign assistance, and even in these countries (with the possible exception of El Salvador) it is most unlikely that moral pronouncements and threatened aid-related sanctions can have much effect.[23]

In Africa, where aid dependency is greater, national and racial sensibilities are perhaps even more intense than in Latin America, and therefore U.S. human rights concerns can be expressed only in even less officious and threatening ways. Policies that in effect encourage offending states to seek rapprochement with the Soviet Union—which has already made considerable inroads into the continent—serve neither the cause of human rights nor U.S. interests.

The United States is at a critical juncture in its international human rights policies. One reason is its relationship with the People's Republic of China, whose systematic violation of human rights is attested to by its very leaders.[24]

The euphoria generated by the newly established "China connection" led a great number of otherwise sober analysts to anticipate "liberalization" on the mainland. But recent evidence indicates that Communism in China today is little different from the Communism that has endured there for over three decades. The PRC is as "unfree" today as in the past. The temporary "liberalization" that saw the explosive growth of "big character posters" and the appearance of the "democracy wall" in Peking has been forcibly suppressed. "Dissident" publications have been universally banned. The news media are rigorously controlled, and "foreign interference" has been systematically eliminated. Unknown numbers of political prisoners still languish in "thought reform" enclaves throughout mainland China.

The United States has decided that relations with the PRC serve certain strategic, political, and economic purposes. But such a relationship should not convey the impression that Washington acquiesces to the human rights behavior of the Peking regime. Any such suggestion could only further erode the thin credibility of America's proclaimed concern for the human rights of all peoples.

Peking, for its part, has never hesitated to admit that its relationship with the United States is dictated by strategic and tactical considerations. Its leaders have regularly asserted that they consider the United States one of the foremost "imperialist oppressors" in the modern world.[25] The U.S. government might be expected to be no less forthright and candid in its assessment of human rights violations in the PRC.

The leaders in Peking have indicated that they anticipate nothing more than cosmetic changes in party policies.[26] The hegemonic role of the Party, the command structure of the economy, and the ideocratic convictions of the Communist leaders make it likely that the PRC will continue the systematic denial of civil and political rights to its people now and in the foreseeable future—whatever the relationship between Peking and Washington.

The human rights issue is the litmus test of ultimate political compatibility. It identifies the Republic of China on Taiwan and every similarly disposed regime as allies in the struggle for human liberty. And it reveals that ideocratic systems—those that share the enduring attributes of the PRC, the Soviet Union, Communist Cuba, the Socialist Republic of Vietnam, and other similarly constituted Marxist regimes—are the principal adversaries of human rights as those rights are understood in the West.

Whatever the temporary political accommodations dictated by immediate circumstances, there is a distinction between political communities that are intrinsically committed to providing civil and political liberties and those that are fundamentally opposed to providing them. This basic distinction helps us sort out real or potential allies from adversaries. By this measure, the Republic of China on Taiwan, irrespective of its present treatment by Washington, remains a critical ally of the United States and other Western nations in the pursuit of enhanced human liberty. Its accomplishments in providing social and economic benefits are now generally acknowledged.[27] Its steady progress in providing civil and political liberties should be celebrated as well.

# Human Rights Practices in the People's Republic of China and the Republic of China, 1982

*The U.S. Department of State is required to prepare for the Congress an annual report of the status of human rights in all nations that receive U.S. assistance and in all others that are members of the United Nations. The following reports on the People's Republic of China and the Republic of China on Taiwan are reprinted from "Country Reports on Human Rights Practices for 1982," published in February 1983. The introduction to this volume explains that the reports draw on information furnished by U.S. missions aboard, congressional studies, non-governmental organizations, and human rights bodies of international organizations. Statistical data on economic and social conditions are from World Bank figures.*

*The introduction states that human rights can be grouped into two broad categories: "(1) the right to be free from governmental violations of the integrity of the person — violations such as killings, torture, cruel inhuman, or degrading treatment or punishment; arbitrary arrest or imprisonment; denial of fair public trial; and invasion of the home; and (2) the right to enjoy civil and political liberties, including freedom of speech, press, religion, and assembly; the right of citizens to participate in governing themselves; the right to travel freely within and outside one's own country; the right to be free from discrimination based on race or sex." The "Country Reports" follow this division: "After an introduction, the description of conditions in each country is divided into two sections which correspond to these two categories of rights. A third section describes the government's attitude toward outside investigations of internal human rights conditions, while a fourth section discusses general economic and social conditions in the country."*

China's government is controlled by elements of the Communist Party, which is the source of all political authority and decision-making in the country. China has a long tradition of authoritarian rule and reliance on laws only to discipline unruly elements. Chinese emperors in successive dynasties, lasting until 1911, ruled by fiat, but their decisions were moderated by Confucian principles. Moreover, central control was often weak and did not extend to the local level, which was dominated by the landed gentry.

The Chinese Communist Party, founded in 1921, has combined Chinese tradition with Leninist principles and methods of well-disciplined political organization and party control over the political, economic, and social life of the country. In practice, however, Mao Zedong's dominance of the party for most of the period from the Long March of the mid-1930's until his death in 1976 often departed from these principles and disrupted the political process.

During the Cultural Revolution period (1966-76), a breakdown of central authority and the dispersion of political power to a number of groups not earlier involved in politics were accompanied by a major intensification of human rights violations. Millions of people were victimized by or enlisted in sometimes violent political campaigns, as the "class struggle" advocated by Chairman Mao was vividly enacted. As central control was reasserted, actual administrative responsibility was borne for a time by the Chinese military. China, however, remains unusual among communist countries in the degree of political involvement by groups and individuals outside the core of the party leadership. At the same time, notwithstanding the existence of several small non-communist parties which have little influence, any alternative to one-party communist rule has been rigidly excluded throughout the period since 1949.

Since 1976, the Chinese system has been in a period of transition and experimentation. The political authorities are moving away from many aspects of the Soviet model that previously guided their political and economic decisions. They are beginning to institute a functioning legal system, though the degree of independence it will be afforded remains to be seen.

Within the Communist Party, power is divided among a group of top leaders in several key organizations, including the Political Bureau and its Standing Committee, the Secretariat, and the Military Commission. Despite his semi-retirement, Deng Xiaoping remains China's most influential policy-maker. China's leaders continue to justify their policies in terms of Marxist-Leninist ideology and the writings of Mao Zedong, but are careful to note that doctrine must be adapted to Chinese realities and that ideological tenets must be applied in the light of current conditions. This more pragmatic attitude has, in recent years, resulted in more flexible economic policies in both industry and agriculture aimed at rewarding individual initiative, while preserving the basic framework of a controlled economy, including common ownership of land and factories.

108

Since Mao's death, the attention of the Chinese government has focused primarily on economic development and the restoration of political and social order.   In an attempt to deal with the pervasive apathy and cynicism toward the Communist Party after the chaos of the Cultural Revolution, China has begun to develop institutions which the Government states are designed to allow broader participation in the political process, and which the Communist Party also hopes will mobilize popular support and enthusiasm for its reform program.   These institutions include the National People's Congress, the Chinese People's Political Consultative Conference, and workers' congresses.   Under the new state Constitution, the Congress's power to supervise other branches of the Government was strengthened at least in a formal sense.   The Constitution envisions multiple candidate local elections, and experiments have already begun.   The practical effect of these developments is not yet known.

China's contacts with the outside have increased considerably in recent years, with tens of thousands of Chinese traveling abroad to study, conduct business, or visit relatives, while even greater numbers of foreigners have visited China. Emigration controls have also loosened significantly.   Chinese can and do listen to the Voice of America and other foreign radio broadcasts.   Cultural life, while still heavily regulated by the party, has become somewhat more lively and features some types of entertainment that are devoid of political content.

While hundreds of churches, mosques, and temples have opened their doors for the first time since the early sixties, believers are excluded from the Communist Party and must exercise restraint in propagating their faith and in their contacts with foreign religious organizations.   Much of the activity of these official religious organs is aimed at regaining central control over local informal religious groups, such as house churches, that have proliferated since the mid-1970's.

Per capita income reached record levels in 1981 to stand at $230.   Economic development strategy has turned to favor production of farm products and consumer products, both of which are now far more readily available than three or four years ago.   Party leaders at the highest level recently have urged improvement in the living and working conditions of intellectuals, who were victims of past discrimination but whose talents are essential if China is to develop.

Though the overall trend has been generally towards a more open society, the political structure has continued to impose significant restrictions on individual rights and freedom. The regime does not tolerate fundamental criticism of the Communist Party and the socialist system and tends to deal harshly with those who voice such criticism.   Contacts with foreigners are subject to monitoring by an extensive formal and informal security network; Chinese not related to foreigners and whose occupation does not require such contacts may be warned or, in extreme cases, arrested if they persist in such contacts.   Writers have been assured that exaggerated government criticisms of the past would not be repeated.   At least one prominent writer criticized in 1981 for anti-government writing has continued to publish after making a self-criticism.   Nevertheless, artists and writers must be cautious in criticizing flaws in the regime and the socialist system so as not to suggest that these are the by-product of socialism or the party leadership.

During 1979, 1980, and 1981, Chinese authorities conducted
extensive and effective campaigns against unauthorized
publications, including wall posters, and arrested scores of
dissidents involved in their promulgation. One person, Wei
Jingsheng, was given a highly publicized -- though not public
-- trial, an event that evoked some domestic support for Wei,
who was sentenced to 15 years in prison. Since that event,
authorities have promulgated "labor education" regulations
which permitted dissidents to be sentenced to labor camps
without benefit of a trial. The fact that these anti-dissent
campaigns were not repeated in 1982 can be attributed not to a
softening of official attitudes, but to the effectiveness of
the 1979-81 drives, which largely succeeded in silencing the
small dissident movement (whose active adherents probably
numbered several hundred). In addition to removing these
persons from the political scene, these campaigns dried up
important unofficial sources of information about human rights
conditions.

China's human rights record in 1982 had ups and downs within a
longer-term positive trend since 1976. In general, there
remains gradual movement towards a more open society, coupled
with continuing harsh controls on fundamental dissent. In the
latter area, perhaps the most noteworthy event of the year was
one that did not happen: there was continued official silence
about the disposition of the scores of dissidents and others
-- including Catholic clergymen arrested in Shanghai in
November 1981 -- who were detained in the preceding three
years. In 1982, Chinese authorities continued to monitor
carefully their citizens' contacts with foreigners. In June,
an American teacher in Beijing and her Chinese fiance were
arrested. The teacher was charged with illicit activities
designed to procure classified documents and expelled from
China. Her fiance apparently remains incarcerated. There
were also reports from several universities that Chinese
students and faculty members who had what authorities deemed
too much contact with foreign teachers were given warnings.

Despite the trend towards loosening controls on foreign travel
by Chinese citizens, regulations promulgated in 1982 make it
more difficult for some university students to study abroad.
New rules prohibit students from accepting private sponsorship
(except from relatives) for their studies abroad and require
them to work in China for at least two years after graduation
before applying to go abroad.

In one area, China moved to facilitate Chinese-foreign
contacts. Regulations requiring all foreigners to obtain
permits in advance in order to travel to any city or district
in China were relaxed in October 1982. Foreign visitors with
a Chinese visa may now travel by air or rail, without further
formalities, to 29 major cities and tourist spots.

In 1982, China mounted a campaign against economic crime and
passed regulations allowing for swifter and more severe
punishment of those convicted of smuggling, bribery, and such
offenses. In January 1983, a local party official was
executed for embezzlement and bribe-taking as part of this
campaign. Similar regulations passed in 1981, applying to
other types of serious crimes, were carried out in several
cases in 1982. In one instance, five armed men who attempted
to hijack a domestic airliner were tried, sentenced to death,
and executed within five weeks of the incident.

China made progress in 1982 in reestablishing a formal legal
system which had been abandoned during the Cultural
Revolution. A new state Constitution, which is the fourth

since 1949, provides for a formal structure in which political power is dispersed and contains provisions to protect the right of the individual to protest arbitrary official action. A new Communist Party constitution promulgated in 1982 also contains provisions designed to prevent over-concentration of power and emphasizes intra-party "democracy." Again, whether these measures will have a significant practical effect cannot now be determined, given that both constitutions continue to emphasize the primacy of the Communist Party. Personnel shakeups in 1982 effectively continued the earlier trend of separating formerly overlapping party and government functions, apparently to give government officials clearer authority to deal with the problems of policy implementation, while the Communist Party continues to formulate basic policy.

In other legal developments, the first civil procedure law in the history of the People's Republic of China (PRC) was promulgated for provisional use in 1982, filling a major gap in the legal system. The Government announced that over 300 laws and regulations, most of them in the economic area, have been implemented since 1979, when the drive to establish a functioning legal system began. The use of mediation committees -- informal groups of laymen who resolve about 90 percent of China's civil disputes and some minor criminal cases, at no cost to the parties -- continued to expand in 1982. There are over 800,000 such committees, in both rural and urban areas.

China's new economic policies allow individuals to have more voice in what they produce and in the quantity of output. In 1982, the Government announced that 90 percent of China's rural production teams (the basic unit in the commune) had adopted "responsibility systems" which allow individuals or groups to make their own production decisions once state quotas are met. Free markets, where goods outside the quota system may be sold at market prices, are a common feature throughout China.

In 1982, in keeping with the "united front" policy aimed at boosting friendly relations between China and Chinese who live overseas, the Government announced that it had released several hundred Kuomintang prisoners, all of those still incarcerated following the civil war in the 1940's.

The long-term trend of human rights in China for the foreseeable future will depend on the political situation. If China's leaders stick to their present course, emphasizing economic development -- including the policy of opening to the outside -- there are reasonable prospects for a continued relaxation of controls in some areas, although the ban on fundamental political dissent will continue and any threat to the preeminence of the Communist Party will not be tolerated.

1.  Respect for the Integrity of the Person, Including Freedom from:

    a.  Killing

There have been no allegations of political killings in China in the recent past, though many were killed or died as a result of violent political struggle during the Cultural Revolution. At present, two members of China's "Gang of Four" (deposed leaders who were prominent during the Cultural Revolution) are under sentence of death, which -- unless commuted -- would be carried out in January 1983. Although the trials appeared to be highly political, Chinese authorities assert that these and others sentenced for Cultural Revolution-era activities were convicted of specific crimes, such as murder and treason, and not for errors of political judgment.

b. Disappearance

There is little information available on the whereabouts of those dissidents arrested in the 1979-81 period. The Government has actively sought to rehabilitate many victims of the Cultural Revolution, but the whereabouts and fate of some remain unknown.

c. Torture

In the aftermath of the fall of the so-called Gang of Four in 1976, it was revealed that the use of torture to extort confessions had been common during the Cultural Revolution (1966-1976), and a government report stated that 10,000 persons were prosecuted in 1980 for violations of citizens rights, including torture, occurring in 1979 and 1980. Official law and regulations now forbid the use of torture. Whether torture has in fact been eliminated is unclear, but there were no reports of torture reaching the US Government in 1982.

d. Cruel, Inhuman, or Degrading Treatment or Punishment

Chinese authorities continued in 1982 an anti-crime drive begun in 1981, emphasizing the need for prompt and severe punishment for those convicted of particularly heinous crimes of violence. In certain cases, after defendants were convicted, a separate "sentencing meeting" was held, attended by thousands of people. The principal purpose of such meetings was to make a public example of the defendant, since sentence had been passed at the trial. The accused would be publicly denounced, and his death sentence revealed. The defendant would then be led out of the rally and executed forthwith; pictures of the entire proceedings sometimes appeared in public court notices announcing the disposition of the case. Since information on such sentencing meetings is not regularly and systematically published by the Chinese, it is impossible to estimate how many might occur each year. On the basis of sketchy information, the approximate order of magnitude was probably around a few hundred.

Current information about conditions in penal institutions is sparse. Inmates are expected to work, and penal authorities have indicated that the value of their labor is sufficient to pay the expenses of their incarceration. In a Beijing prison visited with official sanction by foreigners, inmates live in a crowded but sanitary environment. In penal labor camps, some located in remote areas of China, conditions probably vary widely, and there have been reports of beatings in some camps, and restrictions on letters and family visits. In 1981, China passed regulations allowing authorities to cancel urban residency permits for recidivists and those who escape from prison. Such persons, when their prison terms are over, may have no realistic alternative to remaining in the prison area as contract laborers.

The number of prisoners now held in labor camps is unknown, and estimates in the past varied considerably, including some ranging upwards of 100,000. It appears that the number has diminished significantly in recent years, due both to the "reversals of verdicts" of thousands of prisoners sentenced during the Cultural Revolution and earlier, and to natural attrition.

e. Arbitrary Arrest or Imprisonment

Chinese law provides that a detained person should be released, on the request of himself or his family, if the police have not followed proper arrest procedures. In practice, however, this proviso apparently is rarely, if ever, invoked. There is no provision for preventive detention. A suspect can be held for up to two months before being charged with a crime, though this period may be extended with the approval of higher authorities.

Under "labor education" regulations, those who commit "minor theft or fraud" or who have been expelled from their work units may be sentenced without trial for up to four years of labor. This regulation has been used with some frequency against political dissidents. Sentences are handed down by a public security unit, in consultation with representatives of local civil affairs and labor offices.

f.  Denial of Fair Public Trial

Criminal defendants in China have the right to counsel, and it is provided at little or no cost. Normally, however, the defense attorney enters the case only after the prosecutor has completed his investigation and the defendant has been indicted. In practice, Chinese trials resemble sentencing hearings, where defense representatives plead for clemency for their clients, whose guilt, with very few exceptions, is not contested. The trials are preceded by extensive pretrial investigation, and it is assumed that any individual who is brought to trial is considered to be guilty. Chinese authorities have indicated that the conviction rate of those tried for criminal offenses is about 98 percent.

Defendants in criminal cases may appeal both verdicts and sentences to the next higher level courts, normally the provincial high court. In the few cases where results have been publicized, appeals have sometimes resulted in reduced sentences for the accused.

There are no standing special political or security courts, though a special court was created to handle the "Gang of Four" trial. Although in theory China's courts are independent of party influence, in practice the party undoubtedly stage-manages trials having political significance, such as the "Gang of Four" trial and follow-up trials involving "gang" supporters.

The criminal procedure code requires that all trials be held in public, except those involving state secrets, juveniles, and "personal secrets." In practice, attendance at public trials requires an admission ticket, obtained from organizations selected by the authorities.

2.  Respect for Civil and Political Rights, Including:

a.  Freedom of Speech and the Press

The Constitution guarantees freedom of speech and the press, but in practice open criticism of Communist Party rule and the socialist system is not permitted. The 1979-81 suppression of unofficial publications succeeded in virtually eliminating the publication of dissident views. Many of the authorized periodicals and newspapers are published by the Communist Party, and all others, as well as radio and television broadcasts, are under tight party control.

In this context, open criticism of improper policy implementation by government and party officials -- usually low or middle ranking -- is permitted and practiced by many newspapers. It is assumed that this criticism is controlled and used by the party for its own objectives. "Letters to the Editor" columns are popular features; such letters are often inspired by the party to trigger investigations of alleged injustices. In 1982, the highest ranking figure criticized in the national press was a Vice Minister of Chemical Industries, alleged to have been involved in a bribery scheme.

Access to foreign books and artistic works is sharply limited by the authorities. Foreigners living in China receive materials from abroad uncensored or can purchase them locally with foreign exchange. Foreign periodicals and magazines are available to selected Chinese citizens, primarily in universities. Millions of Chinese read the "Reference News," an officially-controlled selection of translations from the foreign press, subject to censorship.

Foreign journalists resident in China have on occasion been criticized by the authorities for their coverage of sensitive topics, such as the manuscript attributed to dissident Liu Qing in 1981.

> b.   Freedom of Peaceful Assembly and Association

The Constitution guarantees the rights of assembly and association, but in practice these rights are severely circumscribed. Although contacts between Chinese and foreigners in China have increased considerably in the past four years, the authorities closely scrutinize such associations.

The labor union structure is controlled by the Communist Party. The All China Federation of Trade Unions enrolls about half of the urban workforce. The primary function of unions is to foster labor discipline and enhance productivity. Unions do not engage in collective bargaining, and almost never exercise their constitutional right to strike -- a right specifically mentioned in the previous constitution but deleted in the new one. Unions also perform a variety of social and welfare functions.

Worker congresses have now been established in many enterprises. All candidates to these congresses require party approval. These representative bodies in some cases have the authority to elect minor plant officials. The assemblies, which operate under the leadership of the party, serve only an advisory role. China has a great number of professional and other types of associations, such as the Chinese Writers' Association, the All China Youth Federation, and the All China Sports Federation. These groups operate with official sanction, and, in nearly all cases, are controlled by a party committee within the particular association.

> c.   Freedom of Religion

The new Constitution states that citizens of the PRC enjoy freedom of religion and should not be compelled to believe or disbelieve, nor should they be discriminated against for belief or disbelief in religion. This improves upon the previous documents that gave preference to practitioners of atheism by granting them alone the right of propagation. The Constitution assures state protection of legitimate religious activities; illegitimate activities are defined as those that are counter- revolutionary, disruptive of public order, harmful to the health of the people, obstructive of education, or dominated by any foreign country.

In actual practice, religious activities have increased
significantly in the past four years.  Over 200 churches are
said to be open.  According to some official estimates, there
are as many as four million Christians in China.  Unofficial
estimates are markedly higher.  A Catholic seminary opened in
Shanghai in 1982, joining the already established Protestant
seminary in Nanjing.  There are several hundred mosques for
over 13 million Muslims.  Buddhist monasteries have resumed
activities and have ordained small groups of novice monks and
nuns on several occasions since 1979.  There has been
considerable work done on the renovation of Lamaistic
monasteries in Tibet's three major towns since a reform
program in Tibet was launched by Hu Yaobang and Wan Li's trip
there in May 1980.  In contrast to this, village level
monasteries, which were closed and turned into other
facilities such as grain storage warehouses during the
cultural revolution, are apparently not being reopened.  While
the number of practicing monks has increased over the last two
years, they are relatively few in number, closely controlled,
and seem to be playing a largely showcase role.  The
government seems to be feeling its way on this score.

On the other hand, persons with religious beliefs are not
allowed to join the Communist Party.  They are also excluded
from many of the material, career, and other benefits which
often accrue to party members and from effective political
power or participation in China.  The stated aim of the eight
"patriotic" officially-sanctioned religious organizations is
to ensure that all religious organizations accept the
leadership of the party and the state.  Chinese authorities
periodically criticize "feudal superstitious activities," a
description which appears to encompass many traditional
Buddhist and Taoist practices but does not appear to be
directed at Christian and Muslim activities.  In some areas,
authorities actively discourage persons under 18 from
attending religious services.  Many churches, mosques, and
other shrines have reopened since the Cultural Revolution, and
in some areas local governments have assisted with their
refurbishment.  However, some religious property remains
occupied by military and other units.

Chinese authorities carefully monitor and control contacts
between Chinese and foreign religious organizations out of
traditional concern over divided loyalties.  Relations with
the Vatican continue to be strained, partly because of the
Vatican's continued recognition of the claim of the
authorities in Taiwan to be the Government of China.  Equally
important, the officially sanctioned Catholic Church in China
does not recognize Vatican authority.  A group of Catholic
clergy and laymen loyal to the Vatican arrested in Shanghai in
1981 remain incarcerated, as does Bishop Gong Pinmei, who has
been in detention since the mid-1950's.  Contacts with other
foreign groups are allowed to a greater extent.  A small group
of Chinese Muslims has made the pilgrimage to Mecca annually
in recent years.

    d.  Freedom of Movement within the Country, Foreign
       Travel, Emigration, and Repatriation

Travel within China is subject to numerous restrictions.
Chinese citizens must have the permission of their work unit
(expressed in a letter of introduction) in order to buy
airline tickets, secure hotel accommodations, or acquire
ration coupons which allow them to purchase basic food items
in areas outside their place of residence.  Those traveling by
rail who plan to stay with relatives need not obtain a letter
of introduction, but still are required to register with local
police during their visit.  In practice, many Chinese citizens

travel frequently within the country, and some ignore the bureaucratic requirements without reprisals.

Chinese controls over travel abroad and emigration have relaxed signicantly in the past few years. Tens of thousands of Chinese citizens go abroad each year to study, conduct business, or visit relatives. The US Embassy and consulates in China issued around 16,000 nonimmigrant visas in fiscal year 1982 and turned down many thousands of other Chinese applicants who had secured travel documents from Chinese authorities but failed to meet US visa standards. During the same period, 8,000 US immigrant visas were issued in China, with about 70,000 on the waiting list.

Despite the trend towards loosening controls on foreign travel by Chinese citizens, regulations promulgated in 1982 make it more difficult for some university students to study abroad. New rules prohibit students from accepting private sponsorship (except from relatives) for their studies abroad and require them to work in China for at least two years after graduation before applying to go abroad. Chinese citizens cannot travel abroad as a matter of right, and many who apply for passports are refused, though no statistics are available.

Since normalization of US-China relations in 1979, several hundred Chinese residents regarded as local citizens by Chinese authorities have presented claims of American citizenship; in nearly all cases where their claims were valid they have been allowed to leave China under Chinese documentation. In the US-China Consular Convention, both sides agreed to facilitate the reunion of families and to facilitate the travel of persons who may have a claim simultaneously to both nationalities.

There is no practice in China of revoking the citizenship of political dissidents.

China has provided resettlement opportunities to large numbers of refugees, most of them ethnic Chinese from Southeast Asian countries. There have been two large waves. In the early 1960's, 60,000 people resettled in China in the wake of anti-Chinese riots in Indonesia. Since 1977, China has accepted more than 250,000 refugees from Vietnam and about 3,000 refugees from Laos. The number of new refugees dwindled to an estimated 1,000 in 1982. There were no known cases of repatriation of refugees, either forced or voluntary.

Chinese citizens cannot freely move their residences about inside the country. Chinese are registered as residents of a particular locality and cannot change their residence without approval from the authorities, which would normally be granted only for reasons related to the resident's employment. There are many examples of Chinese working couples who live apart (except for holiday visits) because they are unable to get permission needed from the various bureaucracies involved (work units, public security offices) to live together.

e. Freedom to Participate in the Political Process

Effective political participation takes place only within the Communist Party. There are no officially-tolerated opposition parties or groups nor do there appear to be any unofficial ones, due to the effective anti-dissent campaigns of the recent past. Within the Communist Party, "democratic centralism" prevails, which means that policy is made at the top by a few leaders and transmitted downward. In principle, strict discipline is demanded, so that political debate and conflict can take place only by informal mechanisms. There has in the past been significant contestation between groups in the party's top leadership.

Eight other parties exist in China and can make recommendations on behalf of their supporters, but they are very small and have no real effect on political, economic, or social decisions.

Local assembly elections held in 1980 and 1981 provided the first opportunity for Chinese citizens to elect representatives directly in contests where there were at least two candidates, as required by law. In most cases, the local Communist Party heavily influenced the selection of candidates. In a few instances, however, avowedly non-Marxist candidates won elections, some of which were then set aside by party authorities. The Government has claimed that 30 percent of the victors in the elections were not members of the Communist Party.

China's National People's Congress meets for only about two weeks a year to approve government policies, which, in turn, have been mandated by the Communist Party. The National People's Congress has never rejected a government policy, though some have been modified as a result of Congress concerns. While there is sometimes informal dissent from policy, there has never been a significant number of votes cast in opposition.

China has traditionally been a male-dominated society, and men continue to dominate the political process. There are very few women at the top party and government levels. For example only four of the 41 ministers of the central Government are women. Participation by women increases on lower levels; about 20 percent of the deputies elected to local assemblies in 1981 were female, according to government reports.

Minority ethnic and religious groups in border areas such as Xinjiang, Xizang (Tibet), Guangxi, Inner Mongolia, and Yunnan are permitted a limited degree of local autonomy, official recognition of their languages, and favorable treatment in areas such as admission to colleges. The new state Constitution stipulates that either the chairman or the vice chairman of the standing committees of people's congresses in autonomous regions, prefectures, or counties should be a member of the nationality group exercising limited autonomy in that particular area. However, actual political power continues to rest with the party leadership whose leading members are virtually always ethnic Han Chinese. Friction between Han Chinese and minority groups continues in various areas. The governments of the autonomous regions have not interfered with massive Chinese immigration to some areas, which has greatly changed their ethnic balance. The Chinese Government has attempted, thus far without success, to persuade the Dalai Lama to return to Tibet from exile.

3.   Government Attitude Regarding International and Non-governmental Investigation of Alleged Violations of Human Rights

China is a member of the UN Human Rights Commission and the UN Commission on the Status of Women. China has not been the subject of investigations or other human rights actions by official international organizations.

According to press reports, a group of Hong Kong student leaders visited Beijing in May 1982 to discuss the fates of dissidents arrested in 1981. They were received by government representatives, but given little information. Chinese officials have not responded to requests from Amnesty International for meetings and information regarding human rights conditions. Amnesty International's concerns as stated

in its 1982 report for calendar year 1981 are the imprisonment
of dissidents and their detention without trial.  Freedom
House describes China as "not free" and gives it a "6" rating
on a descending scale of one to seven for both political and
civil liberties.

There are no known organizations within China monitoring human
rights conditions.

4.  Economic, Social, and Cultural Situation

China faces massive problems in meeting the basic needs of one
billion people.  The Government has succeeded in providing
basic nutrition, health care, and education.  The average life
expectancy of 68 years is very high for a country that ranks
in the bottom half of developing countries in per capita
income.

Basic health care is available at no or modest cost to Chinese
citizens.  Urban standards of health care are significantly
better than those in rural areas, as reflected in the
different infant mortality rates -- an estimated 12 per 1,000
in cities, as compared with 25 per 1,000 in the countryside.
The Chinese Government has promulgated regulations which
strongly discourage parents from having more than a single
child.  Through the use of social pressure and economic
incentives and disincentives affecting material benefits such
as pay and rations, it has succeeded in reducing the
population growth rate from 2.0 percent in 1970 to 1.5 percent
in 1981.  In response to population control pressures, some
families with too many children or who hold to the historic
value system honoring males but scorning females have resorted
to the practice of infanticide.

The Chinese citizenry enjoys a simple but adequate diet.  Some
basic food items, such as grains and cooking oil, are
rationed.  According to the World Bank, China's calorie supply
exceeded nutritional requirements by about four percent in
1979.  Flexible economic policies in rural areas in recent
years have resulted in the growth of free markets and have
increased the quantity and variety of foods available to
consumers.  Previous discrimination against those with suspect
backgrounds, including intellectuals and former capitalists,
has been curtailed.  In fact, party officials at the highest
levels recently have urged improvements in the living and
working conditions of intellectuals, whose talents are
essential if China is to develop.

The increase in Chinese per capita GDP from $219 in 1978 to
$268 in 1981 has been accompanied by an increase in the supply
of agricultural and consumer goods, reflecting the
Government's emphasis on the development of agriculture and
light industry.  China's new economic development strategy
represents a fundamental shift away from earlier reliance on
the Soviet model, which stressed rapid growth of heavy
industry and military expenditures.

Money incomes in urban and rural areas increased by an average
of three percent and 16 percent respectively in 1981,
according to official figures.  Real national income growth
was estimated at three percent, with an inflation rate of
about 2.5 percent.  However, many foreign observers believe
that overall inflation was significantly higher.

Housing is crowded and poorly constructed in both urban and
rural areas; rural localities, in particular, frequently lack
basic amenities such as electricity and running water.  Rents
are extremely low, averaging about four percent of an urban
dweller's income and ten percent of a peasant's, though many

peasants own their own homes and thus pay no rent.
Construction of housing units is a priority item in the
Government's econmomic plan.

Unemployment in urban areas is a serious social problem in
China. Youths graduating from high school or leaving at an
earlier stage may have to wait many months or even three or
four years before being assigned jobs. Estimates of urban
unemployment range from four to ten million. To help
alleviate this problem the Government has encouraged
individuals, families, and small groups to set up their own
enterprises, instead of relying on the state for job
assignments. Labor service companies set up in many urban
areas provide loans to help individual and collective
enterprises become established.

China's current goal is to provide universal elementary school
education by 1990. According to a Ministry of Education
announcement in April 1982, this goal has already been
attained in areas containing one quarter of the country's
population (probably encompassing most of the urban areas in
China) and is "nearing completion" in areas with another 60
percent of the population. Although the male-female
enrollment ratio is about even at the beginning of the
educational process, it is in favor of males at ascending
levels. Women reportedly account for about one-quarter of
college students. Ninety-three percent of eligible children
are enrolled in the first grade. Around 30 percent of the
young people in the relevant age group complete high school,
and around five percent of high school graduates attend
college. The adult literacy rate was 76.5 percent according
to the 1982 census.

All land in China is owned by the state or by collective
organizations such as communes. Property such as houses,
particularly in rural and village areas, and consumer goods
such as television sets, radios, sewing and washing machines,
and bicycles can be owned by individuals and passed on to
descendants. The People's Bank of China plans to issue
private bank loans for maintenance and expansion of
residential properties as well as for purchases of higher-cost
consumer durables, on an installment basis.

## TAIWAN

More than thirty years of dynamic economic development
contrasts sharply with the pace of political development in
Taiwan, where the ruling authorities have emphasized stability
rather than change.  Nonetheless, the authorities have created
an array of democratic institutions from village to province
level, with candidates inside and outside the dominant
Nationalist Party.  Actual power, however, remains in the hands
of the small leadership group elected in mainland China before
1945, which came to Taiwan after World War II and controls the
Nationalist Party (Kuomintang), the military, and the executive
bureaucracy.  A high degree of political control is exercised
through the security apparatus, which operates under martial
law provisions enacted in 1949 and which the authorities
justify by the threat of military action or subversion from
mainland China.

The enhancement of human rights is publicly endorsed by the
authorities but remains incompletely realized in Taiwan.
Although individuals may run for elective office, coordinated
opposition activity is greatly restricted.  The publication of
opposition political views is closely controlled and the
activities of outspoken oppositionists are monitored, both at
home and, apparently, abroad.  Native Taiwanese, descendants of
Chinese who migrated from the mainland mostly in the eighteenth
century and who now constitute 85 percent of the population,
dominate the economy but are under-represented within the
ruling elite.  Recent evidence suggests that torture and other
forms of physical intimidation are still occasionally used by
police, but probably are not officially condoned.

Nineteen eighty-two saw the continuation of a slow trend toward
improvement in the human rights situation in Taiwan.  Publication and public expression of oppositionist sentiment have
become gradually freer, although there are still strict limits
to what is acceptable.  The authorities continue to recruit
qualified Taiwanese to fill important economic and political,
military, and security posts, a process which will contribute
to an increased share of political power by the Taiwanese.
With the rise of a prosperous middle class, popular concern
about human rights is increasing.  Despite Taiwan's diplomatic
isolation and concern about the island's future after the pass-
ing of the current President, Chiang Ching-kuo, the outlook for
continued improvement in human rights appears favorable.

1.   Respect for the Integrity of the Person, Including
     Freedom from:

     a.   Killing

No killings for political reasons have been substantiated in
Taiwan in 1982, or indeed in recent years.  However, the murder
in February 1980 of the mother and twin daughters of jailed
oppositionist Lin Yi-hsiung and the suspected murder in July
1981 of a Taiwan-born US resident, Professor Chen Wen-cheng,
are widely believed to have been politically motivated.

     b.   Disappearance

In recent years, there have been no credible reports of persons
being abducted or secretly arrested by the security services.
There are no known terrorist organizations operating on the
island.

120

c. Torture

Taiwan law specifically prohibits the use of torture. The Code
of Criminal Procedure states that an accused shall be "frankly"
examined, but that no violence, threat, inducement, fraud, or
other improper means shall be used. This language is repeated
in the Military Trial Law.

The death in police custody of a Taipei taxi driver, Wang
Ying-hsien, in May 1982 focused public attention on the use of
physical violence by police in interrogating criminal suspects,
a practice many believe police resort to frequently. Wang was
picked up on suspicion of robbing a bank and died while in
police custody. The actual robber was captured a few hours
later and Wang's daughter challenged the police account of
Wang's death. The autopsy report, released on August 20,
confirmed that Wang was beaten but ruled that his death was
caused by drowning in the Hsintien River. Although his death
was officially declared a suicide, five policemen were tried
and convicted for illegally arresting Wang and causing him
bodily harm.

d. Cruel, Inhuman, or Degrading Treatment or Punishment

Imprisonment is the usual form of punishment for both political
and nonpolitical offenders. According to the authorities, nine
executions were carried out in 1981, seven of convicted
murderers, and two of persons convicted of robbery.

Taiwan's civilian prisons are severely overcrowded. In April
1982 the press reported that civilian prisons, built to
accommodate 11,261 prisoners, were then holding 17,162 or 5,901
over capacity. Prisoners are forced to share cramped living
quarters and have fewer opportunities for work, exercise, and
family visits. Overcrowding was partially responsible for
severe rioting which broke out in the juvenile section of
Hsinchu Prison in March 1982.

Conditions in the military prisons administered by the security
police, where political prisoners are confined, are reportedly
less crowded. Prisoners receive the same food as soldiers and
have work and recreation opportunities. Although conditions
for the Kaohsiung-incident prisoners have reportedly improved
since their arrest in 1980, six non-Nationalist Party
legislators charged in July 1982 that these prisoners continue
to be denied access to regular work programs and recreational
activities, are prohibited certain amenities accorded other
prisoners, and are subject to special rules which keep them
separate from one another. A few of the Kaohsiung-incident
prisoners are alleged to still suffer from the effects of
pretrial mistreatment.

There is no known discrimination in the treatment of prisoners
because of class, race, sex, or religion.

e. Arbitrary Arrest and Imprisonment

Taiwan's law of habeas corpus requires that, following an
individual's arrest, the arresting authorities notify in
writing the individual and his designated relative or friend
within 24 hours of the reason for his arrest or detention.
The Code of Criminal Procedure specifies that the authorities
may detain an accused for up to two months during investigation
prior to the filing of the formal indictment, and for up to
three months during trial. During the investigation phase,

however, the prosecuting officer may apply to the court for one extension of two months. The period of detention may also be extended during the time the accused is on trial. In recent cases, including the Kaohsiung incident, the authorities generally have followed the requirements of the above provisions, with exceptions occurring more frequently in the military system.

Major changes in the Code of Criminal Procedure, affecting the rights of criminal suspects, were enacted by the Legislative Yuan in July 1982. Suspects were granted the right to legal counsel during the investigation phase, including the right to have a lawyer present during interrogation by police. This was viewed by legal experts as a positive step in the protection of arrestees' rights. However, despite the opposition of the legal establishment, the press, and many legislators, the authorities also forced passage of changes which allow police to arrest without a warrant anyone they suspect of committing a crime for which the punishment would be five years or more in prison. Police power was further augmented to allow police to call in suspects or witnesses for questioning without a formal summons. The authorities justified the new police powers by insisting that the revisions would only legalize long-standing police practices.

The authorities deny holding political prisoners. They have stated that at the end of 1975 there were 254 persons in prison on sedition charges. Some persons have been released and others arrested since that time, but this is the most recent figure made public by the authorities. In December 1982 the authorities disclosed that 92 prisoners convicted of sedition and related offenses are currently being held in the Green Island military prison, compared with 115 reported to be there by Amnesty International in February 1980. Nearly 20 of these, originally arrested for communist activities, have been imprisoned for more than 30 years and were excluded from a general amnesty in 1975. Many of these prisoners, all in their fifties and sixties, are reported to be in poor health.

Many minor crimes in Taiwan are handled under a statute which empowers the police not only to arrest but also to prosecute and punish offenders. This law sometimes has been used against political activists. A substitute law, long sought by legal reformers, was put forward by the authorities in October 1981 but quickly withdrawn after being publicly criticized by lawyers and legislators. Critics complained that the law was even harsher than the one it was meant to replace, particularly provisions for "educational punishment" in military prisons for those accused by police of disturbing "social peace." In March 1982 the authorities reintroduced the "educational punishment" provisions as a separate "hoodlums" law. Although they withdrew it again in the face of heavy criticism, the authorities have indicated that they still intend to enact a police powers law incorporating "educational punishment."

f. Denial of Fair Public Trial

Taiwan's legal system is based on European and Japanese models which do not incorporate trial by jury. Under a 1980 judicial reorganization, district and high courts were shifted from the control of the Executive Yuan to the Judicial Yuan, for the first time formally separating the courts from the prosecution function. It is generally held in Taiwan legal circles that the change has given the judiciary greater independence of action.

Under martial law, which has been in effect in Taiwan since 1949, civilians who commit certain offenses, including sedition, may be tried in military court. Opposition to basic policy (such as expressing views contrary to the authorities' claim to represent all of China, or supporting an independent legal status for Taiwan) is considered seditious and thus punishable under martial law.

The authorities occasionally transfer "important" civilian cases (involving such crimes as homicide, kidnapping, and armed robbery) to the military courts. The authorities state that the military courts' swifter and generally more severe justice acts as a deterrent to potential criminals. Sentences are reviewed only within the Ministry of National Defense. In May 1982, the case of Li Shih-ko, who confessed to carrying out Taiwan's first armed bank robbery and murdering a policeman, was referred to the military courts for action. Li's trial on May 18 lasted less than two hours and the sentence, death, was carried out eight days later.

Neither civil nor martial law provides the defendant with protection from self-incrimination. Following the July 1982 revision of the criminal procedures code, suspects may for the first time have a lawyer present during interrogation. However, the authorities have indicated that the lawyer's role is to protect his client from mistreatment, rather than to provide legal counsel during questioning. In some cases, windows have been installed in police station interrogation rooms in order that lawyers (or family members) may see the suspect without hearing the questioning.

g.    Invasion of the Home

Physical invasion of the home without a warrant is not a common practice in Taiwan, but does occur on occasion. The Code of Criminal Procedure requires that searches be authorized by warrants, signed by a prosecutor or, during a trial, by a judge. However, exceptions to this rule, previously few in number, were substantially increased by the revision of the code in July 1982. When making warrantless arrests, police may also make necessary searches of person or property without prior authority. Other types of violations of the home, such as monitoring telephone calls, are widely believed to exist.

2.    Respect for Civil and Political Rights, Including:

a.    Freedom of Speech and Press

The Constitution guarantees freedom of speech and the press. These rights are limited, however, by the enforcement of martial law restrictions. Individuals are not free publicly to question the regime's basic political policy of anti-communism and claim to sovereignty over all of China. Persons who speak favorably of communism or the People's Republic of China, or persons (usually native Taiwanese) who question the legitimacy of Taiwan's mainlander authorities by suggesting support for Taiwan independence or self-determination, can expect to be charged with sedition and tried in a military court.

Information brought to light during the investigation of the death of Professor Chen Wen-cheng in 1981 suggests that the security authorities closely monitor political expression, both at home and overseas. During questioning by the security

police immediately prior to his death, Chen was reportedly
confronted with recordings of an international telephone call
between himself in the US and an opposition figure in Taiwan
who was later jailed in connection with the Kaohsiung incident,
and of a speech he gave in Pittsburgh supporting the Kaohsiung
incident defendants.  Although the Taiwan authorities later
denied the existence of the Pittsburgh recording, the dis-
closures sparked a resurgence of allegations that Taiwan agents
carry out a systematic program of surveillance and intimidation
of Taiwanese students on American university campuses who are
suspected of advocating Taiwan independence or self-
determination.  Indeed, Taiwan newspaper articles have noted
the role of Taiwan security service units in the United States
and Japan in monitoring dissident Taiwanese political activities.  Although there have been reports of such surveillance
from several US universities, the Taiwan authorities deny that
they carry out surveillance on American campuses.

Censorship of publications occurs frequently.  It is carried
out through provisions of the publications law which empower
the security police to seize or ban printed material that
"confuses public opinion and affects the morale of the public
and the armed forces."  In 1982, the authorities allowed a rise
in the number of domestic political opinion magazines, the more
popular of which support non-Kuomintang politicians and criticize the party.  One or more issues of several of these were
banned during the year.  Nominally the bans are in reaction to
articles critical of the policies of the authorities or which
discuss sensitive subjects, but they are widely viewed as
tactics of intimidation.  The limits of acceptable political
criticism are not clear-cut.  Even periodicals which are
cautious in their selection of articles for publication have
been banned from time to time.  The ban of a single issue of a
magazine may be followed by suspension of the publication's
license for one year.  In 1982, three magazines received this
punishment.

Books are also occasionally banned by the security police.
Control over the daily newspapers is exercised indirectly,
through guidance from the central authorities' information
office and the Kuomintang, and restrictions on the number of
newspapers.  Nevertheless, newspapers have expanded their
coverage in areas previously forbidden, such as news from
mainland China.  Competition among the island's three
television stations has also led to an expansion of their
coverage of mainland and other sensitive international news,
despite the fact that all three are partially or wholly owned
by the authorities.  Mounting criticism (Kuomintang as well as
non-Kuomintang) of security police censorship, as well as of
other elements of martial law administration, has compelled the
authorities to defend their control apparatus.  In June 1982
the Executive Yuan justified regular "selective postal checks"
as necessary to intercept parcel bombs and illegal correspondence with mainland China.  It was denied, however, that the
authorities monitor telephone conversations.

Foreign publications are available, but are also subject to
censorship by the security police and sometimes pages carrying
articles offensive to the authorities are removed or blacked
out before they are distributed.  Some foreign publications are
available through subscriptions only and are not allowed to be
sold on newsstands.  Occasionally, the credentials of foreign
correspondents are suspended for articles which challenge
important official views or positions.

b.  Freedom of Peaceful Assembly and Association

Freedom of Assembly is guaranteed by the Constitution.  While
assembly for nonpolitical purposes is generally permitted,
public assembly for political purposes, except during elections, is often prevented under martial law provisions.  During
the authorized 15-day campaign periods which preceded island-
wide elections on November 14, 1981 and January 16, 1982, all
candidates, including oppositionists, were allowed to hold
rallies.  Those rallies, however, were closely monitored by the
authorities under the Elections and Recall Law of 1980, which
makes candidates liable for prosecution for "seditious"
statements.

Prior to the authorized campaign periods, some oppositionists
held rallies characterized as "private parties."  The authorities' response was moderate but firm and such "parties" were
peacefully broken up.  The same tactic, used by Kuomintang
candidates, usually drew no response from the authorities.
Planned revisions of the election law announced by the authorities will outlaw the use of "private parties" in future
elections.

There is no tradition of trade unionism in Taiwan, and labor
unions do not exercise significant influence either in the
economic or political sphere.  While labor unions are permitted
to organize, walkouts and strikes are prohibited under martial
law.  Collective bargaining, although provided for by legislation, does not exist.

c.  Freedom of Religion

Freedom to practice religion is guaranteed by the Constitution.  Most Taiwan inhabitants adhere to Confucianism, Taoism,
Buddhism, animism, or a combination of beliefs.  Other reli-
gions include Christianity and Islam.  Some pseudo-Buddhist
sects and Sun Myong Moon's Unification Church have been banned,
due to parents' complaints that these groups were a corrupting
influence on Taiwan youth.  The groups were accused of leading
youth to engage in "abnormal behavior" that involved turning
their backs on their families, shifting their allegiance from
state to church, and actively proselytizing for further con-
verts.  Action was taken on the basis of the police offenses
law, a catch-all statute which allows the police to punish
minor offenders without referral to the courts.

While generally respecting the right to practice religion, the
authorities have brought pressure to bear against religious
organizations they consider to be involved in unacceptable
political activity.  In 1977 the Presbyterian Church in Taiwan
(179,000 members), long suspect for its advocacy of Taiwanese
rights, issued a "Declaration on Human Rights" to which the
church leadership has since repeatedly reaffirmed its commitment.  By calling for Taiwan's transformation into a "new and
independent country," the declaration has placed Taiwan's
Presbyterian leaders (almost all native Taiwanese) in a clear
position of questioning Taiwan's mainlander-controlled political institutions.

Friction between the Presbyterian Church and the authorities
came to a head in 1980 when the church's general secretary,
Reverend Kao Chun-ming, and several other Presbyterians were
convicted in military court of harboring sedition defendant
Shih Ming-te.  While admitting he had assisted Shih, Rev. Kao
denied seditious intent; he declared his religious vocation

precluded his betraying someone who had sought help and permitted him only to advise Shih to give himself up. Although relations between the church and the authorities have relaxed somewhat recently, the authorities continue to monitor church activities closely. The authorities have warned church members to avoid involvement in oppositionist political efforts or Taiwan independence activity.

In 1982 the authorities established a religious council, made up of representatives of the island's major religious bodies, to advise them on church matters. There are fears that the council may be used to justify unpopular official policies. Similar concerns have been expressed about legislation proposed in 1981 to regulate church activities. The proposed legislation is opposed by the island's major religious organizations as a threat to freedom of religion, although the authorities argue that the law is necessary to "define the scope of religion" and to "protect freedom of religion." An additional proposed measure would for the first time place religious educational institutions under the control of the Ministry of Education. The authorities argue that this would improve the quality of instruction and provide accreditation for the diplomas granted by these schools. Critics point out that it would also empower the Ministry of Education to control curricula and to place a military training officer in each school. Although action on these measures has so far been withheld, the authorities have not renounced their intention to enact them.

      d.    Freedom of Movement within the Country, Foreign Travel, Emigration, and Repatriation

The Constitution provides for the freedom to change residence. There is general freedom of internal travel in Taiwan, except to military and other restricted areas. Emigration and private travel abroad have become freer since 1979. After the last calendar day of the year in which they turn fifteen, males may not leave Taiwan until completion of their military service. Since 1980, businessmen have been permitted to travel to and do business directly with certain Eastern European countries. Moreover, it is widely believed that the authorities are willing to overlook some personal travel to mainland China if handled discreetly.

Permission to leave Taiwan may be delayed or withheld for security reasons or because the persons involved have criticized the political establishment. Statistics released by the authorities indicate that in 1980, the last year for which we have figures, 949,306 persons applied for exit permission. Of that number, over 20,000 are reported to have been refused, 327 for security reasons and the rest for unspecified causes.

In general, the authorities recognize the right of repatriation of those Chinese holding Taiwan passports who normally reside in Taiwan. Those issued "overseas Chinese" passports do not automatically have the right to travel to Taiwan for permanent residence. In principle, Taiwan will not authorize the entry of Chinese, even those who have long held Taiwan passports, if they have lived in communist-controlled areas within the preceding five years.

Under its program of assistance to Indochinese refugees, Taiwan, through June 1982, has granted permanent resettlement to more than 4,700 such refugees, nearly all of them ethnic Chinese. It has also provided temporary asylum to nearly 2,000

Vietnamese "boat people" (refugees escaping by boat) awaiting
acceptance by other countries.

e.    Freedom to Participate in the Political Process

Reflecting their claim to be the Government of all of China,
the Taiwan authorities possess an array of political bodies
over and above those which pertain solely to the island of
Taiwan.  The locus of power on Taiwan is the presidency and the
central executive branch.  While representation of native
Taiwanese in local and central legislative bodies has been
increasing, Taiwanese are seriously under-represented in the
powerful executive branch, in which persons who arrived from
the mainland after 1945 hold the most powerful positions.
There have been recent increases in the number of Taiwanese
holding executive branch positions, however.  The Vice
President, about one-third of the cabinet (including the Vice
Premier, the Minister of the Interior, the Minister of
Communications, and three Ministers without Portfolio), and the
Governor of Taiwan, among others, are Taiwanese.  Nevertheless,
critics point out that their power and influence both
individually and collectively are limited.

The most important elective bodies at the central level are the
National Assembly, which elects the President and Vice
President, and the Legislative Yuan, which is the Central
Legislature.  There have been no general elections to these two
bodies since 1948, the authorities taking the position that
such elections cannot be held until they re-establish control
over the mainland.  In October 1982 the Minister of the
Interior explained that if overall elections were held the
winners could not represent all of China, but only Taiwan
province.  Beginning in 1969, "supplementary elections" for
these central bodies have been held to choose additional
representatives from Taiwan and the adjacent islands.  The
advanced age and incapacity of many of the members of the
Legislative Yuan elected on the mainland in 1948 forced the
authorities in 1982 to lower the number of legislators required
for a quorum.  Supplemental legislators elected on Taiwan now
constitute the most active group in the Legislative Yuan.

Since 1950, democratic institutions have been in operation at
the provincial and local levels.  Universal suffrage exists for
all citizens twenty years of age and over.  Elections have been
held regularly for provincial, county and municipal offices,
with Kuomintang candidates competing with independents and
oppositionists.  The Taiwan provincial governor and the mayors
of Taipei and Kaohsiung, however, are appointed by the central
authorities.

Despite the existence of two small, nominal opposition parties,
Taiwan is dominated by one party.  The Nationalist Party has
ruled Taiwan since 1945 and is a "revolutionary" party whose
structure and control mechanisms are based on early Soviet
models.  Party organs exist at all levels of the ruling
structure, as well as in the military, schools, and other
public institutions.  New opposition parties are forbidden
under martial law and candidates who oppose the Kuomintang in
elections run as independents or "non-party" candidates.  Even
though the large majority of candidates elected are from the
Kuomintang, independent candidates, nearly all Taiwanese, have
increasingly been successful in the recent past.  In the

provincial elections in November 1981, a loose coalition of "mainstream non-Kuomintang" candidates won about 30 percent of the votes cast, with non-aligned independents and members of the legal opposition parties winning an additional 10 percent. Independents won a similar share of votes in the previous provincial elections in 1977.

Independents face several disadvantages in the election process. The election law enacted in 1980 generally favors Kuomintang candidates, because its provisions, many of which are ambiguous, are interpreted by the central election committee which is controlled by the Kuomintang. The law forbids the participation of students, formerly a prime source of campaign workers for independent candidates, and allows only officially sponsored rallies in which all candidates participate together in the last few days before an election. Independent candidates are further disadvantaged by press self-censorship. The daily press tends to give little publicity to the views of the independents. Periodicals which publicize the views of independent candidates are subject to frequent censorship by the security police. However, such periodicals were not silenced during the provincial elections in November 1981, as they were during previous elections, and they have since been allowed to increase in number.

Women constitute 48 percent of Taiwan's population. The few laws which discriminate against them relate mostly to divorce issues and inheritance. Nearly 500 women were elected to city and town councils in June 1982, taking about 13 percent of the total seats up for election, while in the December 1980 "national" elections women candidates were the top two vote-getters. Regulations governing elections make some provision for guaranteed minimal representation of women in local and central legislative institutions. Enrollment of women in institutions of higher learning has increased 97 percent since 1952, to 411,000 in 1982. The number of women employed in ministries and other official agencies has increased by 40 percent since 1973. A fledgling women's rights movement is slowly growing.

Taiwan's only non-Chinese minority group is made up of descendants of Malayo-Polynesian immigrants who were already established in Taiwan when the first Chinese settlers arrived. Many of these aboriginal "mountain people," who comprise about one per cent of Taiwan's total population, live on restricted-access reservations, but most must compete with the Chinese majority for educational and job opportunities. There is no official policy of discrimination against the aborigines, and the authorities have instituted educational incentives and other social programs to ease their transition into Chinese society. The barriers created by de-facto cultural and economic discrimination, however, are frequently insurmountable. "Mountain people" are often relegated to low-paying, menial jobs by Chinese employers and many are forced to seek long-term employment overseas as fishermen or laborers. The rapid disintegration of tribal culture and the difficulty of "making it" in Chinese society have produced a general malaise within many aborigine communities, which is the source of the widespread alcoholism and "laziness" sometimes caricatured by unsympathetic Chinese. Special designated seats in both central and provincial legislative bodies are reserved for aborigine representatives.

3.   Authorities' Attitude Regarding International and Non-governmental Investigation of Alleged Violations of Human Rights

The Taiwan authorities on occasion have permitted representatives of international human rights organizations, as well as private individuals interested in human rights issues, to visit Taiwan and meet with appropriate officials.

Taiwan's martial law was the subject of hearings before the Subcommittee on Asian and Pacific Affairs of the House Foreign Affairs Committee in May 1982. Prior to this, four members of Congress issued an appeal to the Taiwan authorities calling for an end to the 33-year-old martial law.

The Chinese Human Rights Association, which in the past has focused its attention primarily on human rights questions in mainland China, has recently devoted more of its efforts to human rights in Taiwan. In 1982, the Association sponsored tours for law-makers and legal experts to examine Taiwan's crowded prisons and established a legal aid service for Taipei residents. The association has also put together a human rights report on Taiwan, which was to be released in late 1982. Freedom House, in its 1982 report, rates Taiwan as "Partly Free."

4.    Economic, Social, and Cultural Situation

Taiwan has established an excellent record of providing for the social and economic needs of its people. In general, the opportunity to participate in economic benefits is available to the population as a whole without discrimination. The per capita gross national product (GNP) in 1981 was over $2,500. Unemployment in the first half of 1982 averaged 1.62 percent. The authorities' fiscal 1983 budget allocated more than 30 percent of the total budget to education, science, culture, and social programs.

Although economic growth has recently fallen short of the spectacular rates achieved earlier (GNP grew at a rate of 3.91 percent in the first half of 1982, compared with the 1969-1979 average rate of 10 percent), the economy remains healthy. The prospects for continuing economic well-being are favorable as the authorities attempt to shift the focus of their export-based economy to high-technology industries.

Taiwan has developed an effective public health program and a system of health stations throughout the island - a total of more than 11,000 medical care facilities. In 1980, Taiwan had more than 7.5 physicians, 6.6 nurses, and 22 hospital beds for every 10,000 persons. Health promotion programs include maternal and child disease control and environmental sanitation. Major epidemic disease has been reduced, although limited outbreaks, such as a surge in polio cases in August 1982, still occur. Because of these public health programs and a generally good diet (per capita daily caloric intake exceeds 2,800), life expectancy has increased to 70 years for men and nearly 75 years for women. Taiwan's birth control efforts have been successful in bringing the birth rate in 1981 down to 1.77. This has been crucial in alleviating population tensions on the island, where the population density per square mile of cultivable land exceeds 5,000.

Education is one of the main concerns of the authorities and the population in general. Statistics show that 90.2 percent of the population over age six are literate. Of school-age children, 99.8 percent are currently in school and free compulsory education is available through junior high school. About 60 percent of junior high school graduates pass examinations and enter three-year senior high and vocational school programs.   Entry into Taiwan's extensive system of higher education is also based on competitive exams, and departures from a strict merit system are almost nonexistent.   In 1982, more than 20 percent of college-age youth were enrolled as undergraduate or graduate students.

# Notes

## CHAPTER ONE

1. Midge Decter, in "Human Rights and American Foreign Policy: A Symposium," *Commentary, 72,* 5 (November 1981), pp. 33-34.
2. A. V. Levontin, *The Myth of International Security* (Jerusalem: Hebrew University, 1957), p. xv.
3. Ibid., pp. 233-37, n. 365.
4. See, e.g., Istvan Kovacs, "General Problems of Rights," in Jozsef Halasz (ed.), *Socialist Concept of Human Rights* (Budapest: Akademiai Kiado, 1966), pp. 9-10, 11, 14.
5. See, e.g., John Chipman Gray, *The Nature and Sources of the Law* (Boston: Beacon, 1963), chap. 5; and Harold J. Berman, *Justice in the USSR: An Interpretation of Soviet Law* (New York: Vintage, 1963), chap. 9.
6. Karl Marx and Friedrich Engels, *The German Ideology* (Moscow: Progress, 1964), p. 357.
7. Ibid., p. 372.
8. Ibid., p. 358.
9. Ibid., p. 389.
10. See ibid., p. 373.
11. Hans Kelsen, "Allgemeine Rechtslehre im Lichte materialistischer Geschichtsauffassung," *Archiv fuer Sozialwissenschaft und Sozialpolitik,* December 1931, p. 476.
12. E. Paschukanis, *Allgemeine Rechtslehre und Marxismus* (Frankfurt: Verlag neue Kritik, 1966; a reproduction of the original Russian edition of 1929), p. 117.
13. Ibid., p. 120.
14. A. J. Wyschinski, "Fragen des Rechts und des Staates bei Marx," in *Sowjetische Beitraege zur Staats und Rechtstheorie* (Berlin: Verlag Kultur und Fortschritt, 1953), p. 15.
15. See John N. Hazard, *Communists and Their Law* (Chicago: University of Chicago, 1969), p. 19.
16. Peter Schmidt, "The Citizen's Freedoms," in Halasz, op. cit., p. 239; see p. 235.
17. Hanna Boker, "Human Rights and International Law," ibid., p. 267.
18. Imre Szabo, "Fundamental Questions Concerning the Theory and History of Citizens' Rights," ibid., p. 81. See also Harris O. Schoenberg, "The Implemen-

tation of Human Rights by the United Nations," *Israeli Yearbook of Human Rights*, 1977, pp. 38-39.

19. See A. James Gregor, "Totalitarianism Revisited," in Ernest A. Menze (ed.), *Totalitarianism Reconsidered* (Port Washington, N.Y.: Kennikat, 1981), pp. 130-45.

20. This concern is given classical expression in James Madison's *The Federalist*, no. 51. The importance of the independence of the judiciary is addressed by the Right Honorable Lord Hailsham, *The Independence of the Judicial Process* (Jerusalem: Hebrew University, 1978). See also United States Supreme Court actions, *Cooper* v. *Aaron*, 358 U.S. 1 (1958), and *United States* v. *Nixon*, 418 U.S. 683 (1974).

21. In this regard see Schmidt, in Halasz, op. cit., p. 237, and Szabo, ibid., p. 80; Donald Barry and Harold Berman, "The Jurists," in G. Skilling and F. Griffiths (eds.), *Interest Groups in Soviet Politics* (Princeton: Princeton University, 1971). Compare article 51 of the 1982 Constitution of the People's Republic of China.

22. See A. James Gregor, "Classical Marxism and the Totalitarian Ethic," *Journal of Value Inquiry*, Spring 1968, pp. 58-72.

23. For example, Stalin held that "according to the tenets of Marxism, the emancipation of the individual is impossible until the masses are emancipated." Josef Stalin, "Anarchism or Socialism," in *Collected Works* (Moscow: Foreign Languages, 1952), *1*, p. 299.

24. Szabo, in Halasz, op. cit., p. 76.

25. "Do We Want Democracy or a New Dictatorship?" in the dissident publication *Exploration*, March 25, 1979; reprinted in *What They Say: A Collection of Current Chinese Underground Publications* (Taipei: Institute of Current China Studies, n.d.), pp. 139, 143, 145, 149.

26. See U.S. Department of State, *Country Reports on Human Rights Practices for 1978*, p. 437.

27. June Teufel Dryer, "Limits of the Permissible in China," *Problems of Communism*, November-December 1980, p. 63; and "Why Can't We Enforce the Law?," *Exploration*, September 1979, reprinted in *What They Say*, pp. 202-14.

28. Hungdah Chiu, "China's New Legal System," *Current History*, September 1980, pp. 29-32.

29. See Hungdah Chiu, "Structural Changes in the Organization and Opertion of China's Criminal Justice System," *Review of Socialist Law*, March 1981, pp. 53-72.

30. Lillian Craig Harris, "Images and Reality: Human Rights and the Trial of the Gang of Four," in James C. Hsiung (ed.), *Symposium: The Trial of the 'Gang of Four' and Its Implication in China* (Baltimore: University of Maryland School of Law, 1981), p. 54; and Hungdah Chiu, "Certain Legal Aspects of the Recent Peking Trials of the 'Gang of Four' and Others," ibid., pp. 27-39.

31. See the reports in *Ming Pao Daily:* February 4, 1981, p. 1; March 7, 1981, p. 1; and August 26, 1981, p. 1.

32. "China," in *Amnesty International Report 1981* (London: Amnesty International, 1981), p. 207. See the Chinese commentary, Chang Pao-en, "Ai-kuo,

fan-kung, min-chu" [Patriotism, anti-Communism, democracy], in *Min-chu ch'ao* [Current democracy], November 16, 1981, p.11

33. See *Amnesty International Report 1981,* p. 211; and *Ming Pao Daily:* March 10, 1981, p. 1; November 15, 1981, p. 1; December 4, 1981, p. 3., December 26, 1981, p. 1.

34. See the English text of his speech, "Changes in 'PRC Constitution' Superficial," in *Inside China Mainland,* November 1981, pp. 1, 5. See also the preamble to the 1982 PRC constitution, in which all these affirmations appear.

35. Ho Wu-shuang and Ma Chun, "A Criticism of the Reactionary Viewpoint of Ch'en T'i-ch'iang on the Science of International Law," in Jerome Alan Cohen and Hungdah Chiu (eds.), *People's China and International Law* (Princeton: Princeton University, 1974), p. 26.

36. Ying T'ao, "Recognize the True Face of Bourgeois International Law From a Few Basic Concepts," ibid., p. 30.

37. Ho Wu-Shuang and Ma Chun, ibid., p. 33.

38. See Lucien W. Pye, "The China Factor in Southeast Asia," in Richard H. Solomon (ed.), *The China Factor: Sino-American Relations and the Global Scene* (Englewood Cliffs, N.J.: Prentice-Hall, 1981), p. 225.

39. See Norma Diamond's discussion in the Introduction to an issue devoted to the economy of Taiwan, *Modern China, 5,* 3 (July 1979).

40. Henry Kissinger, "Morality and Power: The Role of Human Rights in Foreign Policy," *Washington Post,* September 25, 1977.

41. See U.S. Department of State, *Country Reports on Human Rights Practices for 1982* and preceding annual volumes; see also U.S. House of Representatives, Committee on International Relations, *Human Rights on Taiwan: Hearing Before the Subcommittee on International Organizations,* 95th Cong., 1st sess., 1977.

## CHAPTER TWO

1. Kurt Glaser and Stephan T. Possony, *Victims of Politics: The State of Human Rights* (New York: Columbia University, 1979), pp. 13, 14.

2. Robert E. Klitgaard, "Martial Law in the Philippines," mimeographed (Santa Monica: Rand Corporation, 1972), p. 19.

3. "The Lawless Case," *European Convention on Human Rights Yearbook, 5* (1969), para. 28.

4. As quoted in Karl Josef Partsch, "Emergencies Regarding the War and Emergency Clause (Article 15) of the European Convention on Human Rights," *Israeli Yearbook of Human Rights,* 1971, p. 333.

5. U.S. House of Representatives, Committee on Foreign Affairs, *Hearings Before the Subcommittee on International Organizations and Movements,* 93rd Cong., 1st sess., 1973, pp. 290-97.

6. See U.S. Senate, *Emergency Power Statutes, Report of the Special Committee on the Termination of the National Emergency* (September 1973), p. 10.

7. See *ex parte* Quirin, 317 U.S. 1 (1942).

8. See *Maung Hla Ggaw* v. *Commissioner* (1948), *Burma Law Reports,* pp.

764, 766, for a British High Court ruling on "preventive justice" in times of emergency.

9. See *The Palestine Gazett,* no. 1442, September 27, 1945, supplement no. 2, pp. 1055-1109.

10. See Alan Dershowitz, "Preventive Detention of Citizens During a National Emergency," *Israeli Yearbook of Human Rights,* 1971, pp. 296-97.

11. District Court of Tel Aviv, sitting as the Supreme Court, Defence Appeal no. 48/1 and 2, *Hamishpat* [Justice], *3,* as cited in Sabri Jiryio, *The Arabs in Israel 1948-1966* (Beirut: Institute for Palestine Studies, 1969), p. 6.

12. See Ibraham Al-Abid, *Human Rights in the Occupied Territories* (Beirut: P.L.O. Research Center, 1970).

13. See Nadav Safran, *Israel the Embattled Ally* (Cambridge: Harvard University, 1978).

14. See Howard M. Sacher, *A History of Israel: From the Rise of Zionism to Our Time* (New York: Dodd, Mead, 1976).

15. U.N. Document A/925, *Report of the International Law Commission Covering Its First Session, 12 April–9 June 1949,* p. 9.

16. See Ruth Lapidoth, "The Security Council in the May 1967 Crisis: A Study in Frustration," *Israel Law Review, 4* (1969), p. 540.

17. See Arthur Sall, *The UN and the Middle East Crisis, 1967* (New York: Columbia University, 1968).

18. See Abraham S. Becker, *Israel and the Palestinian Occupied Territories: Military-Political Issues in the Debate* (Santa Monica: Rand Corporation, 1971), Rand Report R-882, 15A.

19. See "Israel" in U.S. Department of State, *Country Reports on Human Rights Practices for 1980.*

## CHAPTER THREE

1. Sun Yat-sen, *San-min chu-i* (Taipei: China Publishing, n.d.), p. 129.

2. See Robert A. Dahl, *Polyarchy: Participation and Opposition* (New Haven: Yale University, 1971); Samuel Huntington, "Political Development and Political Decay," *World Politics, 17* (1965), pp. 386-430; and Dankwart E. Rustow, *A World of Nations: Problems of Political Modernization* (Washington, D.C.: Brookings Institution, 1967).

3. For references to this period, see the bibliography for chap. 5 in A. James Gregor with Maria Hsia Chang and Andrew B. Zimmerman, *Ideology and Development: The Economic History of Taiwan* (Berkeley: Center for Chinese Studies, 1981).

4. Harold Z. Schriffrin, *Sun Yat-sen and the Origins of the Chinese Revolution* (Berkeley: University of California, 1968), p. 15.

5. Sun Yat-sen, "The True Solution of the Chinese Question," *Kuo-fu ch'üan-chi* [The complete works of Sun Yat-sen] (Taipei: Kuomintang Party History Committee, 1973), *5,* p. 121.

6. Sun Tzu-ho, "The Political Programs of the *Tung-meng hui,*" *China Forum, 5,* 1(1978), pp. 119-22.

7. Sun Yat-sen, "Min-ch-üan ch'u-pu" [The primer of democracy], *Kuo-fu*

*ch'üan-chi, 1,* pp. 667-750. In 1919 Sun affirmed, "It was only with the appearance of the American Republic that the principle of government for the people appeared in the world. Lincoln said: 'Government of the people, by the people, for the people is the people's government.' Only with this government are the people really the masters of a nation" ("San-min chu-i," ibid., *2,* p. 157).

8. See for example Chih-hsin, "Kuo-hui chih fei-tai-pia-hsing chi ch'i chiu-chi fang-fa" [The non-representative character of Parliament and methods for its correction], *Chien-she, 1,* 4(1919), pp. 721-41.

9. *Chien-she* provided translations of William E. Rappard, "The Initiative and the Referendum in Switzerland," *American Political Science Review, 6,* 3(1912), pp. 345-66, and Delos F. Wilcox, *Government by All the People or the Initiative, the Referendum, and the Recall as Instruments of Democracy* (1912).

10. The *San-min chu-i* was delivered as a series of lectures shortly before Sun's death. See *San-min chu-i* (Taipei: China Publishing, n.d.).

11. See Hu Han-min, "Meng-tzu yü she-hui chu-i" [Mencius and socialism] *Chien-she, 1,* 1(1919), p. 168.

12. Lin Yün-kai, "She-hui chu-i kuo-chia chih chien-she kai-lüeh" [Generalizations concerning the construction of socialist states], *Chien-she, 2,* 1(1920), pp. 69-86.

13. *Declaration of the State of Siege, Taiwan Peace Preservation Command 19 May 1949.* An English translation is available in Peng Ming-min, "Political Offences in Taiwan: Laws and Problems," *China Quarterly,* no. 47 (July-September 1971), p. 472. Invoking the amendment clause of the constitution, the National Assembly in May 1948 had empowered the President to declare martial law at his discretion "during the period of Communist rebellion." See Ch'ien Tuan-sheng, *The Government and Politics of China* (Cambridge: Harvard University, 1950), appendix D. In accordance with the process prescribed in Article 174(1) of the Constitution, the president was empowered to take "emergency measures to avert an imminent danger to the security of the State or of the people . . . without being subject to the procedural restrictions prescribed in Article 39 or Article 43 of the Constitution. . . . . The period of national crisis may be declared terminated by the President on his own initiative or at the request of the Legislative Yuan."

14. *Statute for Punishment of Rebellion* [Ch'eng-ch'h p'an-luan t'iao'li]. The statute and its amendments can be found in Taun Shao-yin (ed.), *Six Statutes and Apposite Commentaries* [Lu-fa p'an-chiai hui-p'ien] (Taipei: n.p., 1972), pp. 1402-5.

15. *Statute for Denunciation and Suppression of Rebels* [K'an-luan chih-ch'i chien-su fei-tieh t'iao-li], in ibid., pp. 1450-52.

## CHAPTER FOUR

1. Chiang Ching-kuo, *The Treatment of Subversion in the ROC* (Taipei: China Publishing, 1978), p. 5.

2. Mao Tse-tung, "Fight for a Fundamental Turn for the Better in the Financial and Economic Situation in China," *New China's Economic Achievements* (Peking: Foreign Languages, 1952), pp. 3, 5, 8.

3. Ralph N. Clough, *Island China* (Cambridge: Harvard University, 1978), p. 7.

4. See Edwin K. Snyder, A. James Gregor, and Maria Hsia Chang, *The Taiwan Relations Act and the Defense of the Republic of China* (Berkeley: Institute of International Studies, 1980), chap. 1.

5. See "PRC Foreign Ministry Statement on Sino-American Talks at Geneva, January 18, 1956," and "Liu Shao-chi's Political Report of the Central Committee of the Chinese Communist Party to the Eighth National Congress of the Party," in Hungdah Chiu (ed.), *China and the Question of Taiwan: Documents and Analysis* (New York: Praeger, 1973), pp. 263, 273.

6. See Hugh Scott, *The United States and China* (Washington, D.C.: Government Printing Office, 1976), p. 3, and reports in the *New York Times*, August 3, 1976. For a more detailed account of the armed engagements in the Taiwan Strait since 1949, see Ti Tsung-heng, "Shui chiang-tsai chin-hou k'ung-chih Taiwan hai-hsia" [Who will control the Taiwan Strait?], pt. 1, and "Kuo-King hai-hsia chan-cheng pi shih-li chien-t'ao" [An examination of the actual force levels in ROC-PRC confrontation in the Taiwan Strait], *Ming Pao Monthly* (Hong Kong), *12*, 2, (February 1977), pp. 20-27.

7. Figures on PRC and ROC military capability are from *The Military Balance, 1981-1982* (London: International Institute for Strategic Studies, 1981). See also Edwin K. Snyder and A. James Gregor, "The Military Balance in the Taiwan Strait," *Journal of Strategic Studies*, *4*, 3 (September 1981).

8. James B. Linder and A. James Gregor, "Taiwan's Troubled Security Outlook," *Strategic Review*, *8*, 4 (Fall 1980).

9. Harlan W. Jencks, "China's 'Punitive' War on Vietnam: A Military Assessment," *Asian Survey*, *19*, 8 (August 1979), pp. 801-15.

10. See A. James Gregor, Introduction to Milos Martic, *Insurrection* (New York: Dunellen, 1975).

11. See Thomas A. Marks, "The Maoist Conception of the United Front with Particular Application to the United Front in Thailand Since October 1976," *Issues and Studies*, *16*, 3 (March 1980), pp. 47-48.

12. See Jane Degras (ed.), *The Communist International 1919-1943 Documents* (London: Frank Cass, 1971), vols. 1 and 2.

13. Marks, op. cit., p. 50.

14. Karl Marx, "The Victory of the Counter-Revolution in Vienna," in Karl Marx and Friedrich Engels, *Collected Works* (New York: International, 1975–), *7*, p. 506.

15. Friedrich Engels, "Kaiserlich russische wirkliche geheime Dynamitraete," in Karl Marx and Friedrich Engels, *Werke* (Berlin: Dietz, 1962), *21*, p. 189.

16. Engels to Vera Zasulich, April 23, 1885, ibid.

17. V. I. Lenin, "Guerrilla Warfare," in *Collected Works* (Moscow: Foreign Languages, 1962), *11*, pp. 213-23.

18. As cited in Jay Mallin (ed.), *Terror and Urban Guerrillas* (Coral Gables: University of Miami, 1971), p. 18.

19. Marks, op. cit., pp. 54-55.

20. Mao Tse-tung, "Report on an Investigation of the Peasant Movement in Hunan," in *Selected Works* (Peking: Foreign Languages, 1967), *1*, pp. 23-59.

21. For a convenient collection of Mao's thought on revolutionary organization and violence, see Jay Mallin (ed.), *Strategy for Conquest: Communist Documents on Guerrilla Warfare* (Coral Gables: University of Miami, 1970).

22. See Fred W. Riggs, *Formosa Under Chinese Nationalist Rule* (New York: Macmillan, 1952), and—for a more colorful account—George H. Kerr, *Formosa Betrayed* (Boston: Houghton Mifflin, 1965). For a later account, see Douglas Mendel, *The Politics of Formosan Nationalism* (Berkeley: University of California, 1970), chap. 2. For a Nationalist Chinese version, see *The Truth About the February 28, 1947, Incident in Taiwan* (Taichung: Historical Research Commission of Taiwan Province, 1967).

23. See Ching-yuan Lin, *Industrialization in Taiwan, 1946-72* (New York: Praeger, 1970).

24. Mao Tse-tung, "Greet the New High Tide of the Chinese Revolution," *Selected Works, 4,* pp. 119-27.

25. King C. Chen, "Peking's Attitude Toward Taiwan," in Hungdah Chiu (ed.), *Normalizing Relations with the People's Republic of China: Problems, Analysis, and Documents* (Baltimore: University of Maryland School of Law, 1978), pp. 39-40.

26. See Chen Cheng, *Land Reform in Taiwan* (Taipei: China Publishing, 1961) and *An Approach to China's Land Reform* (Taipei: Chen Cheng, 1951).

27. See T. H. Shen (ed.), *Agriculture's Place in the Strategy of Development: The Taiwan Experience* (Taipei: Joint Commission on Rural Reconstruction, 1974), and T. H. Lee, *Intersectoral Capital Flows in the Economic Development of Taiwan, 1895-1960* (Ithaca: Cornell University, 1971).

28. See Samuel P. S. Ho, *Economic Development of Taiwan* (New Haven: Yale University, 1978), and Walter Galenson (ed.), *Economic Growth and Structural Change in Taiwan* (Ithaca: Cornell University, 1979).

29. For a more detailed treatment of the various restrictions on the military prosecution of civilians under emergency regulation, see Ku P'o-hsien, *T'ung-yung Fa-lu Chih-shih* [General legal knowledge] (Taipei: n.p., n.d.), pp. 27-28.

30. For a documented discussion of this period, see Mab Huang, *Intellectual Ferment for Political Reforms in Taiwan, 1971-1973* (Ann Arbor: Center for Chinese Studies, University of Michigan, 1976).

31. The article in six installments was unsigned and appeared under the title "The Voice of an Ordinary Citizen" in *Chung-yang jih-pao* [Central daily], April 4-9, 1972.

32. See Jan S. Prybyla, *The Societal Objective of Wealth, Growth, Stability, and Equity in Taiwan* (Baltimore: University of Maryland School of Law, 1978); Wei Yung, "Modernization Process in Taiwan: An Allocative Analysis," *Asian Survey, 16,* 3 (March 1976), pp. 262-63; and John C. H. Fei, Gustav Ranis, and Shirley W. Y. Kuo, *Growth With Equity: The Taiwan Case* (New York: Oxford, 1979).

33. See Gustav Ranis, "Industrial Development," in Galenson, op. cit.

34. *Chung-yang jih-pao,* as cited in Huang, op. cit., p. 91. See also J. Bruce Jacobs, "Taiwan in 1973: Consolidation of the Succession," *Asian Survey, 14,* 1 (January 1974).

35. Recent cases include: (1) In 1978 Wu Chun-fa organized a "Taiwan Free

Republic Revolutionary Committee" with himself as "chairman." Wu attempted to raise funds and distribute propaganda in anticipation of a planned program of revolutionary violence. Riots and attacks against the central police headquarters and the bus stations were planned, as well as armed forays against financial institutions in the city of Kaohsiung. (2) In 1976-77 Tai Hua-kuang organized a "People's Liberation Front" that mailed more than two hundred threatening letters to foreign businessmen in Taiwan in an effort to impair the island's economic stability. Plans were made to place bombs in two Taipei buildings to give substance to the threats, and riots were planned to disrupt public life. (3) In 1977 Wang Hsing-nan was convicted of conspiracy to mail letter bombs to government officials. One of these bombs had seriously injured Hsieh Tung-min, the governor of Taiwan Province. Two other bombs were mailed but were deactivated by authorities.

36. See Steven J. Rosen and Robert Frank, "Measures Against International Terrorism," in David Carlton and Carlo Schaerf (eds.), *International Terrorism and World Security* (New York: Wiley, 1975), p. 68.

37. J. Henk Leurdijk, "Summary of the Proceedings: Our Violent Future," ibid., p. 4.

38. Rosen and Frank, ibid., p. 63.

39. Amnesty International, *Taiwan (Republic of China)* (London: Russell Press, 1976 and 1980).

40. *ROC Position and Attitude Toward Sedition Cases* (Taipei: China Publishing, n.d.), p. 2.

41. See Chen, op. cit., p. 47.

42. Something of the same argument is found in George Lenczowski's assessment of the factors that led to the successful revolutionary overthrow of the regime of the Shah of Iran. According to his account, the security forces of the Shah had allowed the process of revolutionary mobilization to proceed too far to abort the process. "The Arc of Crisis: Its Central Sector," *Foreign Affairs, 57,* 4 (Spring, 1979), pp. 796-820.

43. See the testimony of various witnesses in U.S. Senate, Committee on Foreign Relations, *Hearings: Taiwan* (1979).

44. Clough, op. cit., p. 57.

## Chapter Five

1. *Far Eastern Review,* March 1925, p. 103, as quoted in Gottfried-Karl Kindermann, "The Taiwan Land Reform: Its Ideological Origins and Radical Features," *Asian and African Studies,* 6 (1970), pp. 157-58.

2. The appeal to pluralistic democratic ideals is found not only in the standard government literature but in all of Taiwan's "dissident" press.

3. See Tang Hui-sun, *Land Reform in Free China* (Taipei: JCRR, 1954), pp. 229-31.

4. See Hung-chao Tai, "The Kuomintang and Modernization in Taiwan," in Samuel P. Huntington and Clement A. Moore (eds.), *Authoritarian Politics in Modern Society* (New York: Basic Books, 1970), p. 423.

5. See Martin M. C. Yang, *Socio-Economic Results of Land Reform in Taiwan* (Honolulu: East-West Center, 1970).

6. See Jan S. Prybyla, "Economic Development in Taiwan," in Hungdah Chiu (ed.), *China and the Taiwan Issue* (New York: Praeger, 1979); and Wei Yung, "Modernization Process in Taiwan: An Allocative Analysis," *Asian Survey, 16,* 3 (March 1976).

7. As quoted in *American Foreign Policy: Current Documents* (Washington, D.C.: Government Printing Office, 1962), p. 1185.

8. As cited in Arthur J. Lerman, *Taiwan's Politics: The Provincial Assemblyman's World* (Washington, D.C.: University Press of America, 1978), p. 26.

9. Ibid., p. 67; Tai, op. cit., p. 417.

10. Lerman, op. cit., pp. 49, 51, 57, 65.

11. See Mark Plummer, "Taiwan: Toward a Second Generation of Mainland Rule," *Asian Survey, 10,* 1 (January 1970), pp. 18-24; and the article by Fu Hu in Fu Ch'i-hsuen et al., *Chung-hua ming-kuo chien-ch'a yuan Chih yen-chiu [A study of the Control Yuan of the Republic of China]* (Taipei: College of Law, National Taiwan University, 1957), *3,* pp. 969-1028.

12. See Edward Shils, "Political Development in New States," *Comparative Studies in Society and History, 2* (1959-1960), p. 391.

13. See Edward Shils, "Opposition in the New States of Asia and Africa," mimeographed (Grenoble: International Political Science Association, 1965).

14. Yung Wei, "Political Development in the Republic of China on Taiwan," in Hungdah Chiu (ed.), *China and the Question of Taiwan* (New York: Praeger, 1973), pp. 99-101.

15. See *China Yearbook 1969* (Taipei: China Publishing, 1970); and Richard L. Walker, "Taiwan's Movement Into Political Modernity, 1945-1972," in Paul K. T. Sih (ed.), *Taiwan in Modern Times* (New York: St. John's University, 1973), pp. 373-74.

16. See *Chung-yang jih-pao,* May 30, 1972, p. 1; and Tillman Durdin, "Chiang Ching-kuo and Taiwan: A Profile," *Orbis,* Winter 1975.

17. John Franklin Copper, "Taiwan's Recent Elections: Progress Toward a Democratic System," *Asian Survey, 21,* 10 (October 1981), pp. 1029-39.

18. For a discussion of the *Formosa* affair, see John Kaplan, *The Court Martial of the Kaohsiung Defendants* (Berkeley: Institute of East Asian Studies, 1981).

19. See John Franklin Copper, "Taiwan in 1980: Entering a New Decade," *Asian Survey,* January 1981.

20. For some discussion of the "Kaohsiung Incident" from diverse points of view, see Mary Ellen Leary, "The 'Formosa' Affair," *The Nation,* March 22, 1980; *Myth and Reality of the Kao-Hsiung Riot* (Cambridge, Mass.: China Youth Club, January 30, 1980); "To Heal, Not to Hate: A Report on the Kaohsiung Incident," *Free China Review,* February 1980; reports in the *New York Times,* December 14, 1979, and the *Christian Science Monitor,* December 21, 1979; and "Democracy Goes on Trial With the Dissidents," *Far Eastern Economic Review,* April 4, 1980.

21. *The Supplementary Parliamentary Elections, 1980* (Taipei: Kwang Hwa, 1980), p. 2.

22. *The Public Officials Election and Recall Law* (Taipei: Kwang Hwa, 1980).

23. See Diane Ying, "Bunting and Posters Don't Hide Serious Undertone of Taiwan's Elections," *Asian Wall Street Journal,* December 5, 1980.

24. See *The Supplementary Parliamentary Elections, 1980,* pp. 5-8.

25. See Copper, "Taiwan's Recent Elections."

26. See *China Post,* December 8, 1980; and Paul Wilson, "A Moderately Successful Poll," *Far Eastern Economic Review,* December 12, 1980.

27. *The Supplementary Parliamentary Elections, 1980,* p. 24.

28. Hsü Fu-kuan, *Ju-chia cheng-chih ssu-hsiang yü min-chu tzu-yu jen-ch'üan* (Taipei: Pa-shih nien-tai ch'u-pan-she, 1979).

29. K'ang Ning-hsiang, *Wen-cheng liu-nien* (Taipei: K'ang Ning-hsiang, 1978).

30. Hsieh Cheng-i, *Tang-nei yü Tang-wai* (Taipei: Min-ch'üan t'ung-hsün-she, 1979 and 1980).

31. T'ao Pai-ch'uan, *T'ai-wan yao keng-hao* (Taipei: Shih-pao wen-hua ch'u-pan shih-yeh yu-hsien kung-ssu, 1978 and 1979), *T'ai-wan hai neng keng hao ma* (Taipei: Ching-shih shu-chü, 1970), and *T'ai-wan tsen-yang neng keng hao* (Taipei: Yüan-ching ch'u-pan-she, 1978).

32. New York: Columbia University, 1977; Taipei: Tsung-ch'ing t'u-shu ch'u-pan kung-ssu, 1978.

## CHAPTER SIX

1. U.S. Department of State, *Country Reports on Human Rights Practices for 1979,* p. 526.

2. For a general discussion see Houn Fu-wun, *Chinese Political Tradition* (Washington, D.C.: Public Affairs Press, 1965).

3. Jyh-pin Fa, *A Comparative Study of Judicial Review Under Nationalist Chinese and American Constitutional Law* (Baltimore: University of Maryland School of Law, 1980), pp. 27-39.

4. See Tao Lung-sheng, "Reform of the Criminal Process in Nationalist China," *American Journal of Comparative Law,* 19 (1971), pp. 747-65.

5. Fa, op. cit., p. 103.

6. Ibid., pp. 105-8.

7. Ibid., p. 121.

8. Yao Chia-wên, "P'an-kuo lun" [On sedition], *Mei-li tao, 1,* 1 (August 16, 1979), pp. 61-65.

9. Ho Wên-chên, "T'ai-wan ta ti-chu" [Taiwan's big landlords], *T'ai-wan chêng-lun* [Taiwan political review], no. 3 (October, 1975), pp. 15-19; K'ang Ning-hsiang, "Ju-ho ts'u-chin T'ai-wan ti chin-pu yu ho-hsieh" [How to promote Taiwan's progress and harmony], ibid., no. 1 (August 1975), pp. 5-7; Ch'ên Ta-jên, "Ts'ung T'ai-pei-shih fang-wu ch'i-ch'ê suo-yu-ch'üan k'an suo'tê fen-p'ei wen-t'i" [Looking at the problem of distribution from the ownership of housing and automobiles in Taipei], *Mei-li tao, 1,* 1 (August 16, 1979), pp. 59-60; Huang Shun-hsing, "Wei nung-min ch'üan-i hsiang hsing-chêng-yüan Sun-yuan-chang chih-hsun" [A demand for an explanation on behalf of the peasants' rights and welfare from Premier Sun of the Executive Yuan], ibid., *1,* 3 (October

25, 1979), pp. 35-42; Ch'ien Shang-i, "Man-t'an chung-hsiao ch'i-yeh wên-t'i" [On the problem of the middle and small business enterprises], ibid., *1, 3* (October 25, 1979), pp. 66-67; Chang Yu, "T'ai-wan ching-chi fa-chan ti hui-ku yü chien-t'ao" [A retrospective and an examination of Taiwan's economic development], *Pa-shih nien-tai* [The eighties monthly], *1, 6* (November 1979), pp. 9-11; Li T-ai-yung, "T'ou-shih tang-ch'ien T'ai-wan lao-kung wên-t'i" [A thorough perspective on Taiwan's present labor problem], ibid., *2,* 1 (December 1979), pp. 55-57. All these articles may have influenced the administrative decision to ban the journals in which they appeared. Since no public review of those decisions is allowed, the grounds on which the sanctions were based is difficult to determine.

10. See Szû-t'u Ming-t'ai, "Pa-shih nien-tai T'ai-wan ching-chi ti mu-piao" [The economic objectives of Taiwan in the 1980s], *Pa-shih nien-tai, 1,* 1 (June 1979), p. 5.

11. Ch'ên, op. cit., p. 60.

12. See the discussion in Walter Galenson, "The Labor Force, Wages, and Living Standards," in Walter Galenson (ed.), *Economic Growth and Structural Change in Taiwan* (Ithaca: Cornell University, 1979).

## CHAPTER SEVEN

1. William Barrett, "Human Rights and American Foreign Policy," *Commentary, 72,* 5 (November 1981), p. 26.

2. For a supporting view, see Ernest W. Lefever, "The Trivialization of Human Rights," *Policy Review,* no. 3 (Winter 1978), pp. 11-26.

3. Article 4(2).

4. See Frank Lormier, *The Population of the Soviet Union: History and Prospects* (Princeton: Princeton University, 1946); and William Petersen, *Population* (New York: Macmillan, 1975), p. 675.

5. See Robert Conquest, *The Great Terror* (New York: Macmillan, 1968).

6. For estimates of those who died in the various Maoist campaigns on the Chinese mainland, see Richard L. Walker, *The Human Cost of Communism in China* (Washington, D.C.: Government Printing Office, 1971).

7. Speech of September 28, 1977, in BBC *Summary of World Broadcasts,* FE/5632/C/1.

8. Alexander I. Solzhenitsyn, *The Gulag Archipelago, 1918-1956* (New York: Harper and Row, 1974), chaps. 2, 8-10.

9. Sun Yat-sen, "To Build a New Nation Requires the Realization of the Three Principles of the People" [Yü kai-tsao hsin-kuo-chia tang shih-hsing san-min chu-i], *Küo-fu chüan-chi, 2,* p. 508.

10. Sun Yat-sen, "San-min chu-i," Essay of 1919, *Küo-fu chüan-chi, 2,* p. 157.

11. Sun Yat-sen, "The Three Principles of the People and the Future of the Chinese People" [San-min chu-i yü chung-kuo min-tsu chih ch'ien-tu], *Kö-fuchüan-chi, 2,* p. 205.

12. See Herbert J. Ellison, "Human Rights East and West," in Raymond D. Gastil (ed.), *Freedom in the World: Political and Civil Liberties 1978* (London: G. K. Hall, 1978), particularly pp. 75-76.

13. See Montek Ahluwalia, "Income Inequality: Some Dimensions of the Problem," in Hollis Chenery et al., *Redistribution With Growth* (Oxford: Oxford University, 1974).

14. "In terms of income distribution, Taiwan society is extraordinarily equalitarian." U.S. Department of State, "Taiwan," *Country Reports on Human Rights Practices for 1980*.

15. Peter T. Bauer, *Dissent on Development* (London: Weidenfeld and Nicolson, 1971).

16. See Robert T. Holt and John E. Turner, *The Political Basis of Economic Development: An Exploration in Comparative Political Analysis* (Princeton: Van Nostrand, 1966), pp. 50-61.

17. See Seymour Martin Lipset, *Political Man: The Social Bases of Politics* (New York: Doubleday, 1963), particularly p. 64.

18. See Samuel P. Huntington, "Political Development and Political Decay," *World Politics, 17*, 3 (April 1965).

19. David Apter, *The Politics of Modernization* (Chicago: University of Chicago, 1965), p. 40.

20. See Erik Thorbecke, "Agricultural Development," in Walter Galenson (ed.), *Economic Growth and Structural Change in Taiwan* (Ithaca: Cornell University, 1979); and H. S. Tang and S. C. Hsieh, "Land Reform and Agricultural Development in Taiwan," *Malayan Economic Review, 6*, 1 (April 1961).

21. Gustav Ranis, "Industrial Development," in Galenson, op. cit.

22. U.S. Department of State, "Taiwan," *Country Reports on Human Rights Practices for 1980*.

23. See Bryce Wood, "Human Rights Issues in Latin America," in Jorge I. Dominguez et al., *Enhancing Global Human Rights* (New York: McGraw-Hill, 1979), pp. 186-87.

24. "Purging the Unrepentant," *People's Daily*, July 23, 1979; Yeh Chien-ying, chairman of the Standing Committee of the National People's Congress, "Speech at the Celebration of the Thirtieth Anniversary of the Founding of the People's Republic of China," as translated in *Inside China Mainland, 1* (November 1979), pp. 1-6; see also "The Meaning of the 'Legal Reform,'" *Ming Pao Daily*, November 1, 1981.

25. See the declaratory policy of Peking in King C. Chen (ed.), *China and the Three Worlds* (White Plains, N.Y.: M. E. Sharpe, 1979).

26. "Holding Fast to the People's Democratic Dictatorship Is an Immutable Political Principle," *Kuang Ming Daily*, April 23, 1981, as translated in *Inside China Mainland, 3* (June 1981), pp. 1-5.

27. See John C. H. Fei, Gustav Ranis, and Shirley W. Y. Kuo, *Growth With Equity: The Taiwan Case* (New York: Oxford University, 1979); and A. James Gregor with Maria Hsia Chang and Andrew B. Zimmerman, *Ideology and Development: Sun Yat-sen and the Economic History of Taiwan* (Berkeley: Center for Chinese Studies, 1981).

# Index of Names

# CENTER REPRINTS AND ESSAYS

**Reprints are $1 each. Postpaid if payment accompanies order.**
**Orders of $20 or more, 10 per cent discount.**